THE OFFICIAL GUIDE

TOM YOHE & GEORGE NEWALL

HYPERION
NEW YORK

KNOWLEDGE IS POWER!

Executive Producer: Tom Yohe
Producers: George R. Newall and Radford Stone
Music Director: Bob Dorough
Based on an Idea by David B. McCall

Photo on p. x by Ron Breland

Library of Congress Cataloging-in-Publication Data

Newall, George
    Schoolhouse rock! / George Newall and Tom Yohe. — 1st ed.
       p.   cm.
    ISBN 0-7868-8170-4
    1. Schoolhouse rock! (Television program)   I. Yohe. Tom. 1937– II. Title.
PN1992.77.S35N48   1996
791.45'72—dc20
                                      95–42116
                                         CIP

First Edition

10 9 8 7 6 5 4 3 2 1

INTERIOR DESIGN & PRODUCTION BY ROBERT BULL DESIGN

D E D I C A T I O N

To David B. McCall, mentor and friend,
who asked us to share his brilliant idea.
And then was generous enough
to let us take it and run with it.

CONTENTS

America Rock

Science Rock

INTRODUCTION

We didn't know. ABC didn't know. Not even David McCall, who had the idea in the first place, knew. Who *could* have known that our innocent lyrics and simple pictures would burn themselves into the consciousness of a generation considered unfairly by most to be *unconscious*: Generation X. But now you can sit at your restaurant table, look up at your twenty- or thirty-something waiter or waitress, say "Conjunction Junction," and chances are you'll get the same enthusiastic reply every time: "What's your function?"

The fact is, our innocent little lyrics and pictures made literally *billions* of TV impressions between 1973 and 1985. (A TV "impression" being defined as one show, seen by one viewer, one time.) The little three-minute capsules appeared as many as seven times each weekend. How does a bill get through Congress? Why is Zero a hero? What are the words to the preamble to the Constitution? How many planets are in our solar system? Why are we all "victims of gravity"? We answered all these questions and more over and over again for thirteen continuous years.

According to an article in Indiana University's *Indiana Daily Student*, "The *Schoolhouse Rock* video clips on ABC Saturday morning television were more than booster shots in grammar, multiplication, American history and science. For thirteen years, the videos were to the 'baby bust' (those born from 1965–1975) what Howdy Doody was to the baby boom: an icon."

But in all those years there was little or no feedback from those of you who were spending your "wonder years" glued to the television set. From adults, yes. The Television Academy would favor us with an Emmy every other year. (We seemed to be taking turns with *Sesame Street*, which we thought put us in pretty good company!) Various governmental and lobbyist groups requested cassettes of "I'm Just a Bill" to use in their training programs for staffers. The University of Michigan Medical School and Columbia College of Physicians and Surgeons called to ask for "Telegraph Line" to help introduce the nervous system to first-year medical students.

Oh sure, every now and then someone would report hearing "Lolly, Lolly, Lolly" or "Interplanet Janet" being whistled in the supermarket. But when the series "wound down" in the mid-eighties, there wasn't a single peep from the millions of kids still camped in front of their television sets. By then, those of you who had gotten the heaviest dosage of *Schoolhouse Rock* in the seventies and early eighties had entered high school and college and, in all likelihood, were "busy" sleeping until noon on Saturdays!

GRAMMAR ROCK
THOMAS G. YOHE, EXECUTIVE PRODUCER
RADFORD STONE, PRODUCER

I want to thank all the little people who made this possible

Emmy winners again!
(The second Emmy.)
From left to right: Radford Stone, George Newall, David McCall, and Tom Yohe

Jack Sidebotham's quick doodle on the original winning Emmy card.

The animation cels were thrown out. Musical arrangements were misplaced. And the original 24-track recording tapes were stored in a barn in Connecticut. Who knew?

Occasionally, a few of you popped up and tugged at our shirttails. Someone writing a college thesis on "The Effect of Television on Juvenile Sensitivities" somehow tracked us down asking for a firsthand history of *Schoolhouse Rock*. Naturally, we obliged, flattered that someone had remembered.

Then in the late eighties the calls became more frequent—once every other month instead of twice a year. An undergraduate at the University of Connecticut began a nationwide petition campaign to try and convince ABC that *Schoolhouse Rock* belonged back in their Saturday morning schedule. Another devotee traveled from campus to campus collecting signatures on his petition, frequently calling both us *and* ABC with progress reports from phone booths along the way.

Bob Dorough, traveling in Europe with his jazz trio, started getting requests from expatriate American students asking for their favorite *Schoolhouse Rock* songs.

Then, in the spring of 1990, we were asked to participate in a senior symposium on education at Dartmouth College. On a Saturday night in April, the largest auditorium on campus was filled with 900 rocking, rolling, clapping, foot-tapping *Schoolhouse Rock* fans.

Gee, suddenly it looked like a whole bunch of someones remembered *Schoolhouse Rock*. And it began to dawn on us that our little educational sideline had made a lasting and positive impact on millions of young minds.

The inspiration for *Schoolhouse Rock* was born on horseback while our boss, David B. McCall, then president of McCaffrey and McCall Advertising, was vacationing with his family at a dude ranch in Wyoming. David noticed that son Davey, who was having more than his share of trouble learning the multiplication tables in school, could sing any Rolling Stones lyric, chapter and verse. In fact, any rock lyric at all! Hmmm, thought Dad, if Davey could only remember rote *learning* as well as he does rote *rock* . . .

Back from vacation, David told us about his idea. He then asked a jingle writer who'd composed a lot of catchy music for the agency's commercials to come up with something suitable for an educational phonograph record. The result was not at all what David had in mind. Something halfway between the saccharine sweetness of "The Singing Lady" and "Bryllcreme, a little dab'll do ya!"

We decided to look for a different kind of composer. Someone more off-beat and less inhibited by the usual songwriting formulas.

It just so happened George knew about Bob Dorough, a wonderful jazz pianist and composer with a penchant for turning mundane subjects into marvelous music. From "Do Not Remove This Tag," inspired by one of those everpresent mattress labels, to "Love" (Webster's definition), a lyric that includes the fact that in tennis, "love" means "no points are scored and you have nothing!"

We met with Bob. David explained his idea. And several weeks later, after immersing himself in his daughter's math textbooks, Bobby returned to regale us with "Three Is a Magic Number." We were completely blown away. Astonished. Astounded. Bob had taken the number three and twisted and turned it so many ways that it had truly been transformed into "a magic number."

David, who happened to be on the board of New York's Bank Street College of Education, arranged to have them test recordings of "Three Is a Magic Number" in several urban and suburban school districts. Teachers reported back enthusiastically. Not only was "Three Is a Magic Number" an efficient remedial tool for the "Daveys" of the world, it was also a magical way to introduce young minds to the multiplication tables in the first place.

Bob's lyrics were so visual that Tom decided they would make a wonderful educational film. He designed a magician character and drew a storyboard of "Three Is a Magic Number." Radford Stone, a colleague of ours and the account executive on the agency's biggest account, the ABC Television Network, saw the storyboard and—knowing that ABC was on the lookout for some "pro-social" children's programming—suggested we take the idea to ABC.

Rad set up a meeting with the network's young Vice President for Children's Programming, Michael Eisner. (Yes, *that* Michael Eisner!) Mike invited the legendary animator Chuck Jones of *Roadrunner* and *How the Grinch Stole Christmas* fame to join our meeting. Chuck was producing an anthology show for ABC called *Curiosity Shop,* and Mike thought a segment called *Multiplication Rock* might fit right in. We played Bob's demo tape and presented our storyboard, frame by frame. At song's end, Mike turned to Chuck and said, "What do you think?" Chuck's reply: "Buy it!"

And that's how easy it is to get into show business!

The next three years would prove that Bob Dorough's imaginative handling of the three-times table was no fluke. Bob became our Mozart of multiplication, imbuing each of the tables with its own unique character and easy-to-grasp concept. From the two-by-two loading of Noah's Ark in "Elementary, My Dear" to the "Dek, El, Do" toe counting in "Little Twelvetoes," Bob composed and arranged every single note—and sang most of them, as well!

In turn, Tom's advertising background and experience with storytelling visualization transformed Bob's words. His designs for "Three is a Magic Number," "Ready or Not, Here I Come," "I Got Six," "Figure Eight," and "My Hero, Zero" confirmed Chuck Jones's enthusiastic endorsement. And remember, we still had our day jobs as co-creative directors of McCaffrey and McCall Advertising. So the designs and layouts were pretty much done at home on the kitchen table at night.

Schoolhouse Rock has always been defined by the disciplines of advertising: vivid concepts, artfully framed in a very limited amount of time. So it's no accident that so many of the other designers who contributed (George Cannata, Bob Eggers, Paul Frahm, Lew Gifford, Paul Kim, Phil Kimmelman, Bill Peckmann, Arnold Roth, Jack Sidebotham, Rowland Wilson) share an advertising background.

This held true for our composers, as well. When it came time to tackle the parts of speech, we recruited Lynn Ahrens, then a fledgling copy department secretary at McCaffrey and McCall, to write us a song about nouns. "A Noun Is a Person, Place, or Thing" became one of sixteen songs Lynn would compose for us even as she was moving up from secretary to copywriter to jingle writer to very successful Broadway composer (*Lucky Stiff*, *Once on this Island*, and *A Christmas Carol* in collaboration with Alan Mencken). Kathy Mandry, another of our copywriters, collaborated with Bob on "Rufus Xavier Sarsaparilla," as did Tom on "Sufferin' Till Suffrage." George composed music and lyrics on "Unpack Your Adjectives," "The Energy Blues," and "Them Not-So-Dry Bones." And then there was Bob's close friend and frequent collaborator, Dave Frishberg. Dave's first effort was "I'm Just a Bill" and his "sad little scrap of paper" drawn by Tom and given a distinctive voice by Jack Sheldon became one of the most endearing of the original *Schoolhouse Rock* songs.

Speaking of Jack Sheldon, he was part of *Schoolhouse Rock*'s jazz connection. Yes, it's called Schoolhouse *"Rock,"* but Bob never felt confined by one style of music. As a result he let each individual concept dictate what kind of music should frame the lyric. However, being a jazz musician himself, he tended to look for talent within that genre. What resulted were vocals by Blossom Dearie ("Figure Eight" and "Unpack Your Adjectives"), Grady Tate ("I Got Six," "Naughty Number Nine," and "Fireworks"), and a list of well known sidemen that included Sheldon, Frishberg, Tate, Steve Gilmore, Bill Goodwin, Dick Hyman, Hubert Laws, Zoot Sims, Stuart Scharf, Ben Tucker, and Bernard Purdy.

Of course, when it came to educational validity, we never had the presumptuousness to fly by the seat of our pants. We've been lucky enough to collaborate with educational consultants who share our view that learning doesn't have to be dull. From Dorothy Bloomberg at the Bank Street College, who convinced Michael Eisner that, yes, *kids* would understand what *adults* couldn't in "Little Twelvetoes"; to *Science Rock* consultant Professor Emeritus Gil Dyrli at the University of Connecticut whose student organized the national petition drive that spread from campus to campus and helped bring *Schoolhouse Rock* back from network oblivion in 1992.

Even today, bulletin boards on computer on-line services are filled with enthusiastic endorsements from teachers all over the country. Yes, you *can* learn the preamble to the Constitution from a three-minute animated cartoon!

But even with all the hard work by all the talented people, who would have known that *Schoolhouse Rock* would become a TV icon remembered in the same breath with *The Brady Bunch, Sesame Street,* and *Scooby Doo*?

Who would have known? We guess *you* would have known. After all, you do remember that six times eight is forty-eight, a noun is a person, place, or thing, and that "We are all endowed with cetain unalienable rights."

Indubitably!

Tom Yohe
George Newall

Multiplication Rock

Developed in Consultation with Bank Street College of Education

MY HERO, ZERO

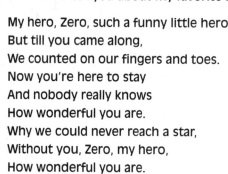

SYNOPSIS

Emerging from a telephone booth, a pint-sized, superhero Zero gets wrapped up in his cape and spirals skyward atop a star. In the process, he illustrates for his skeptical older sister that nothing is important, nothing is something, and we could never go anywhere without taking nothing along.

A Saint Bernard comes to the rescue, and the little Dutch Boy plugs up the dike with his thumb. Two cavepeople discuss the object in front of them: "A wheel?" "No, a zero." Zero raises the speed limit from 6 to 60 mph. And the weight of his barbells increases from 5 to 50 to 500. Clunk!

Zero?

Yeah, Zero is a wonderful thing.
In fact, Zero is my hero!

How can Zero be a hero?

Well, there are all kinds of heroes, you know.
A man can get to be a hero
For a famous battle he fought . . .
Or by studying very hard
And becoming a weightless astronaut.

And then there are heroes of other sorts,
Like the heroes we know from watching
    sports.
But a hero doesn't have to be a grown-up
    person, you know,
A hero can be a very big dog
Who comes to your rescue,
Or a very little boy who's smart enough to know what to do.

But let me tell you about my favorite hero.

My hero, Zero, such a funny little hero,
But till you came along,
We counted on our fingers and toes.
Now you're here to stay
And nobody really knows
How wonderful you are.
Why we could never reach a star,
Without you, Zero, my hero,
How wonderful you are.

What's so wonderful about a zero?
It's nothing, isn't it?

Sure it represents nothing alone . . .

But place a zero after 1
And you've got yourself a 10.
See how important that is?
When you run out of digits,
You can start all over again.
See how convenient that is?

That's why with only 10 digits including zero,
You can count as high as you could ever go . . .
Forever, towards infinity,
No one ever gets there, but you could try.

With 10 billion zeroes,
From the cavemen till the heroes,
Who invented you,
They counted on their fingers and toes
And maybe some sticks and stones, or rocks and bones,
And their neighbors' toes.
You're here,
And nobody really knows
How wonderful you are.
Why we could never reach the star,
Without you, Zero, my hero,
Zero, how wonderful you are.

Place one zero after any number
And you've multiplied that number by 10.
See how easy that is.
Place two zeroes after any number
And you've multiplied that number by 100.
See how simple that is.
Place three zeroes after any number
And you've multiplied that number by 1,000.

Et cetera, et cetera, ad infinitum, ad astra, forever and ever
With Zero, my hero, how wonderful you are.

TRIVIA

Schoolhouse Rock premiered on the weekend of January 6–7, 1973, with "My Hero, Zero," "Elementary, My Dear," "Three Is a Magic Number," and "The Four-Legged Zoo."

Everyone who had worked on the songs and animation attended a Saturday-morning "premiere party" at George and Boni Newall's apartment in Manhattan.

Despite the more melancholy nature of this tune, "My Hero, Zero" ranks among the top ten favorites of all *Schoolhouse Rock* songs.

FACTS

First Aired in 1973
Lyrics and Music by Bob Dorough
Performed by Bob Dorough
Designed by Tom Yohe
Animation by Phil Kimmelman and Associates

ELEMENTARY, MY DEAR

SYNOPSIS

Standing in the pouring rain and wearing matching yellow raincoats, a bearded Noah shares an umbrella with his son on the S.S. Ark. With the boat perched precariously on Mt. Ararat, Dad explains the two-times table using the dozens of paired animals marching from the boat.

Forty days and forty nights,
Didn't it rain, children.
Not a speck of land in sight,
Didn't it, didn't it rain.
But Noah built the ark so tight
They sailed on, children.
And when at last the waters receded
And the dove brought back the olive tree leaf,
He landed that ship near Mt. Ararat
And one of his children grabbed Noah's robe and said,
"Hey, Dad, how many animals on this old ark anyway, huh?"

Elementary, my dear, 2 x 2 is 4.
Elementary, my dear, 2 x 3 is 6.
Elementary, my dear, 2 x 4 is 8.
Elementary, my dear, 2 x 5 is 10.

2 x 1 is 2 of course.
And it must occur to you,
You get an even number
Every time you multiply by two.

Elementary, my dear, 2 x 6 is 12.
Elementary, my dear, 2 x 7 is 14.
Elementary, my dear, 2 x 8 is 16.
Elementary, my dear, 2 x 9 is 18.

2 x 10 is 20, 11 twice is 22.
Double 12, that's 24, 13 twice is 26,
14 twice is 28, 15 twice is 30, now you build it up on 30,
16 twice is 32, (clap clap) elementary . . .
17 twice is 34, (clap clap) elementary . . .
18 twice is 36, (clap clap) elementary . . .

19 twice is 38, (clap clap) elementary . . .
20 twice is 40, and it must occur to you,
You can double any number,
All you do is multiply by two . . .

Elementary, my dear, 2 x 2 is 4. (Woo!)
Elementary, my dear, 2 x 3 is 6. (Yeah!)
Elementary, my dear, 2 x 4 is 8. (Whoop!)
Elementary, my dear, 2 x 5 is 10. (Yeah!)

Now if you want to multiply 2 x 174,
Or some big number like that.
2 x 174 equals 2 x 100 plus 2 x 70 plus 2 x 4
That's all.
So 2 x 174 equals 200 plus 140 plus 8 . . . or 348.
It's elementary.

Elementary . . . elementary . . .

Twice 32 is 64, (clap clap) elementary . . .
Twice 33 is 66, (clap clap) elementary . . .
Twice 34 is 68, (clap clap) elementary . . .
Twice 35 is 70, (clap clap) elementary . . .
Yeah, yes, it's elementary, yeah.

Now, what's 2 x 98?

Aw! That's hard!

No, it's very simple.
2 x 98 equals 2 x 100 minus 2 x 2.
That's 200 minus 4 . . . 196.
Elementary.

Forty days and forty nights
Didn't it rain, children.

TRIVIA

Bob Dorough's original "demo" had no reference to Noah and the Ark. Tom Yohe made the suggestion in an effort to make it easier for Jack Sidebotham to visualize the lyrics. (Sidebotham also designed "Bert and Harry Piel" for Piels beer, a very popular series of animated commercials that ran in the New York area in the fifties and early sixties.)

The songs that make up *Multiplication Rock* were originally recorded for an album by the same title, for which Bob Dorough received a Grammy nomination in 1974. To this day, Dorough is often asked to sing *SR* songs at his performances, and has even been hired to perform *SR* songs at wedding receptions!

FACTS

First Aired in 1973
Lyrics and Music by Bob Dorough
Performed by Bob Dorough
Designed by Jack Sidebotham
Animation by Focus Design, Inc.

THREE IS A MAGIC NUMBER

SYNOPSIS

In this mystical song a magician leads you through the three-times table. The past, the present, and the future are depicted as the Wright brothers' airplane, a jumbo jet, and a spaceship (respectively), and Faith, Hope, and Charity are all women in seventies garb. Then, of course, there is the happy family of three running through the countryside.

In this spot, "3" shows up as a triple-decker ice cream cone and as the jersey numbers on ten football players coming out of the locker room. (Remember #30 breaking through the doorway?)

Three is a magic number,
Yes it is, it's a magic number.
Somewhere in the ancient, mystic trinity
You get three as a magic number.

The past and the present and the future.
Faith and Hope and Charity,
The heart and the brain and the body,
Give you three as a magic number.

It takes three legs to make a tripod
Or to make a table stand.
It takes three wheels to make a vehicle
Called a tricycle.

Every triangle has three corners,
Every triangle has three sides,
No more, no less.
You don't have to guess.
When it's three, you can see
It's a magic number.

A man and a woman had a little baby,
Yes, they did.
They had three in the family,
And that's a magic number.

3-6-9, 12-15-18, 21-24-27, 30.
3-6-9, 12-15-18, 21-24-27, 30.
Multiply backwards from 3 x 10:
3 x 10 is 30, 3 x 9 is 27, 3 x 8 is 24, 3 x 7 is 21,
3 x 6 is 18, 3 x 5 is 15, 3 x 4 is 12,
And 3 x 3 is 9, and 3 x 2 is 6,
And 3 x 1 is 3 of course.

Now dig the pattern once more:
3 . . . 3-6-9
12 . . . 12-15-18
21 . . . 21-24-27 . . . 30

Now multiply from 10 backwards:
3 x 10 is 30 (Keep going), 3 x 9 is 27, 3 x 8 is 24, 3 x 7 is 21,
3 x 6 is 18, 3 x 5 is 15, 3 x 4 is 12,
And 3 x 3 is 9, and 3 x 2 is 6.
And 3 x 1 . . .
What is it?!
Three!
Yeah. That's a magic number.

A man and a woman had a little baby,
Yes, they did.
They had three in the family,
That's a magic number.

TRIVIA

This very first *SR* tune was written as a song for an educational record, but its visual lyrics became the inspiration for the series of short segments that became *Schoolhouse Rock*.

In its original recording, "Three Is a Magic Number" stretched longer than the 2 minutes 58 seconds limit, so a stanza was spliced out of the song when it went to television. The same was done with "My Hero, Zero." Those who own the *Multiplication Rock* album, however, can hear the songs in their original form.

FACTS

First Aired in 1973
Lyrics and Music by Bob Dorough
Performed by Bob Dorough
Designed by Tom Yohe
Animation by Focus Design, Inc.

THE FOUR-LEGGED ZOO

SYNOPSIS

Six kids and their teacher Miss Simpson take a class trip to the zoo to visit lions, buffalo, and coyotes . . . plus a vicuna, an ibex, and a kudu!

(Drum riff)

We went to the four-legged zoo
To visit our four-footed friends.
Lions and tigers, cats and dogs,
A goat and a cow and a couple o' hogs.
   A rhinoceros and of course a hippopotamus
   And, oh yes, a horse!

   There were elk and bison, a gnu or two,
   Giraffes and elephants, quite a few,
A llama, alpaca, vicuna too,
Zebras, ibexes, and one big kudu.
It was swell.
I liked the gazelle.

Now Miss Simpson said . . .
She teaches school, you know—
Yeah, she took us there.
Well, Miss Simpson said—
If we counted every head on these quadrupeds,
Then multiplied that number by four,
We'd know how many feet went through the door,
If we turned 'em all loose.
Oh no, don't do that!
It's really a groovy zoo.

But anyway, what Miss Simpson said,
It was a good chance to work on our fours in our head.
1-2-3-4!

I'll take a lion . . . 1 x 4
He's got four legs and maybe a roar.
Gimme 2 camels . . . that's 2 x 4
8 legs walking 'cross the desert floor.

A tiger and a lamb and a fat kudu,
Would be 3 x 4 equals 12 legs too.
But we might have to subtract
When that tiger was through! (Rrarr!)

Four 4-footed friends, no matter who,
Would have sixteen legs, and it's always true
That 4 x 4 equals 16,
And 5 x 4 is 20.

Now a coach and six, if you were Cinderella,
Would have you home by midnight
If those twenty-four legs ran fast as light . . .
6 x 4 equals 24 and 7 x 4 equals 28
Anyone knows that, who cares about seven . . .
And eight antelope have thirty-two legs 'cause 8 x 4 is 32.

Here come a small herd of buffalo.
They say they're getting extinct, you know.
I can count nine—that's thirty-six legs.
9 x 4 equals 36.
Here comes a baby buffalo.
That's good! That's ten!
And 10 x 4, you know, is 40.

Eleven coyotes . . . 11 x 4
Went slinkin' over the prairie floor
On all of their legs . . . equals 44.

Now 12 x 4 is as high as we go . . .
12 x 4 equals 48.
But there were so very, very, many, many more
Animals standing there by the gate,
That we'd have to use a pencil if we counted them all.
And we really had fun,
And we saw every one.
A bear, a cougar, a jackal, a yak,
A fox, some deer, and a sweet giraffe.
And I can't remember how many, many more,
But we multiplied them all by four.
And some of them thanked us with a roar.

TRIVIA

Originally, Bob Dorough combined 4, 6, and 8 in one song. But when he was told there had to be a separate song for each number, he got a bit stuck. When he was on a hiking trip with his ten-year-old daughter Aralee and her friend Lisa, they gave him the idea for the title and theme of this song. Both girls sang on the final recording.

FACTS

First Aired in 1973
Lyrics and Music by Bob Dorough
Performed by Bob Dorough
    and chorus of kids
Designed by Bob Eggers
Animation by Phil Kimmelman
    and Associates

READY OR NOT, HERE I COME

SYNOPSIS

As gigantic colored numbers land along the hillside, a red-haired, freckle-faced country bumpkin wearing overalls and a yellow shirt plays hide-and-seek with a bunch of kids.

Now everybody try to find a good hiding place.
This ol' tree is gonna be the base.
I'm gonna close my eyes and hide my face
And count to a hundred by fives.
Ready? Go!

5, 10, 15, 20, 25, 30, 35, 40, 45, 50, 55, 60, 65, 70, 75, 80, 85, 90, 95, 100.
Ready or not, here I come.

Apple, peaches, pumpkin pie.
Who's not ready, holler "I"—("I").
Oh, all right, I'll count it again,
But you better get hid, kid.
Here we go.

5, 10, 15, 20, 25, 30, 35, 40, 45, 50, 55, 60, 65, 70, 75, 80,
85, 90, 95,100,105, 110, 115, 120. There!
A bushel of wheat and a bushel o' rye,
Who's not hid, holler "I."

Twenty nickels makes a dollar!
I didn't hear anybody holler.
5 x 20 is 100,
Everybody got to be hid.
All eyes open, here I come, whew!

Multiplyin' by five is a little like countin' by five. In fact, if you counted along on your fingers as you counted out loud by fives, your fingers would tell you how many fives you've got.

OK let's count together, now.
Count on your fingers . . .
One finger for each count out loud . . .
Get set. Ready? Go!

5, 10, 15, 20—STOP!
Twenty.

You got four fingers, see, that means 4 x 5 is 20.
Let's try another one.
Get set. Ready? Go!

5, 10, 15, 20, 25, 30, 35—STOP!
Thirty-five?
Seven fingers . . . that's right,
7 x 5 is 35.

OK, let's try a longer one. Now when you run out of fingers at 50
—you see, because 10 x 5 is 50—then start over with the same
fingers and remember that you owe 10 . . . Get set. Ready? Go!

5, 10, 15, 20, 25, 30, 35, 40, 45, 50, 55, 60—STOP!
Ten and two, right?
That's twelve fingers.
And 12 x 5 is 60.
See how it works?

Now you may notice that if you multiply five by an even number, your
product will end in zero; and if you multiply five by an odd number,
your product will end in five.

OK, now let's do one more game of counting by fives on our fingers.
This is a long one.
Keep going.
Get set. Ready? Go!

5, 10, 15, 20, 25, 30, 35, 40, 45, 50, 55, 60, 65, 70, 75, 80, 85—STOP!
Eighty-five. Seventeen fingers.
Look at that boy with seventeen fingers stickin' up.
How do you do that, kid?
Anyway, 5 x 17 is 85.

You see, that's three fives short of 100. If you had 3 more nickels,
15 cents, and added the 15 to 85, you'd get 100, right?

'Cause 5 x 20 is 100.
Everybody got to be hid!

It's 5, 10, 15, 20, 25, 30, 35, 40, 45, 50, 55, 60, 65, 70, 75, 80, 85, 90, 95, 100.
Ready or not,
Here I come!

TRIVIA

The inspiration for this jazzy song
came from a two-week family reunion
camp-out in Arkansas. Dorough took
along his electric piano to work on
the *Multiplication Rock* songs, and his
nieces and nephews helped him with
some of the key phrases ("bushel of
wheat and a bushel o' rye . . . Apple,
peaches, pumpkin pie . . . ").

Check out the Camp Yohe and
Camp Newall T-shirts!

FACTS

First Aired in 1973
Lyrics and Music by Bob Dorough
Performed by Bob Dorough
Designed by Tom Yohe
Animation by Phil Kimmelman
    and Associates

I GOT SIX

SYNOPSIS

This bass-driven funky tune features a young black kid and a couple of his friends on the streets of New York City, buying candy and playing jacks.

   Remember the prince with his seventies afro and outfit, and harem girls for wives?

I got six.
That's all there is.
6 x 1 is 6, 1 x 6

He got six.
I put mine with his and we got twelve
6 x 2 is 12, 2 x 6

I got six, you got six,
She got six.
We got eighteen all together.
If we can get 'em all together.
6 x 3 is 18, 3 x 6

I got six in my right hand,
Six in my left hand,
Six on my head.
And you got six in your pocket.
Put 'em all on the floor—that's twenty-four.
6 x 4 is 24, 4 x 6

I got six red hens.
They laid five eggs each.
All the eggs hatched out,
And the yard was full of thirty little chicks.
6 x 5 is 30, 5 x 6

One fine day,
They all started in to lay.
I got thirty-six eggs and I took 'em in the house,
And I put 'em in boxes,
Six eggs each. Six boxes.
Aw, 6 x 6 is 36, 6 x 6

Going to the candy store—
I'll take six of these and six of those
and six of them and six of the others.
And also six of the red, six of the white,
and six of the blue.
Il put 'em in one bag—that's forty-two.
6 x 7 is 42, 7 x 6

Oh, I'm throwin' down jacks,
Pickin' up six.
I made eight tricks
And didn't miss a lick.
6 x 8 is 48, 8 x 6

Nine hungry men had six dollars each
(Aw!) and that's fifty-four bucks,
But they were out of luck.
Cause fifty-four bucks won't buy dinner downtown.
Not for nine.

Then there were six hungry men
They had nine dollars each (Yeah!)
And they went downtown, and the waiter said "Sit down!"
Oh, it makes a big difference how you spread it around.
6 x 9 is 54, 9 x 6

See that prince over there (Yeah!)
The one with the fuzzy hair.
He's got six rings on every finger.
He don't wash no dishes,
Not with sixty diamonds.
6 x 10 is 60, 10 x 6

He brought along eleven camels.
Now, ain't that nice. (Ain't that nice)
Each one loaded down with six casks of oil and spice.
Brought quite a price.
6 x 11 is 66, 11 x 6

He had twelve wives.
He better be rich.
Each one had six kids—six children each.
6 x 12 is 72, 12 x 6

But me, I got six. (I got six)
That's all there is. (That's all there is)
6 x 1 is 6 (6 x 1 is 6)
1 x 6 (1 x 6)

I got six. (I got six)
That's all there is. (That's all there is)

TRIVIA

When Bob Dorough wrote this song, he didn't know what he meant by "I Got Six." Tom Yohe was the one who came up with the idea for six balloons.

In addition to singing this tune, renowned jazz drummer Grady Tate played drums on many of the original *Schoolhouse Rock* recordings.

George Newall, an accomplished jazz pianist himself, used to hang out at The Hickory House in Manhattan to hear The Billy Taylor Trio, which frequently performed there. It was through his friends Ben Tucker (bass) and Grady Tate (on drums) that Newall met Bob Dorough.

FACTS

First Aired in 1973
Lyrics and Music by Bob Dorough
Performed by Grady Tate
Designed by Tom Yohe
Animation by Phil Kimmelman and Associates

LUCKY SEVEN SAMPSON

SYNOPSIS

Happy-go-Lucky Seven Sampson made being bad look good as he tripped his way around the town, making messes and getting into trouble with cops and store owners. With a big "7" on his right foot and a black circle around his left eye, Lucky Seven shows the kids from Public School #7 how to multiply by his favorite number. In the end, he lands safely back in the same Buckeye Produce truck (full of cabbage) that brought him into town.

Now you can call me Lucky, 'cause Lucky's my name.
Singin' and dancin', that's my game.
I never did a whole day's work in my life,
Still everything seems to turn out right.
Like a grasshopper on a summer's day,
I just love to play
And pass the time away,
'Cause I was born 'neath a lucky star.
They said I'd go far.

Makin' people happy, that's my favorite game.
Lucky Seven is my natural name.
Slippin' and slidin' my whole life through,
Still I get everything done that I got to do,
'Cause I was born 'neath a lucky star.

School is where you are?
Aw, that's not hard.
Let me show you something.

You multiply 7 x 1,
I got 7 days to get that problem done.
Multiply 7 x 2,
Take 14 laughs when you're feeling blue.
Multiply 7 x 3,
A 21-day vacation you can play with me.
Multiply 7 x 4,
You got 28 days (that's a one month more)
To pay the mortgage on your store.
Don't worry. Something will turn up!

Multiply 7 x 5,
I don't know how you did it, but man alive, that's 35.

Multiply 7 x 6,
Grab a stick and make a 42 clickety-clicks.
Multiply 7 x 7,
Take 49 steps right up to seventh heaven.
Multiply 7 x 8,
They got 56 flavors and I just can't wait.
Multiply 7 x 9,
63 musicians, all friends of mine.
Multiply 7 x 10,
And that brings you right back to 70 again.

You know, I think that's important.
There's a trick there somewhere.

Multiply 7 x 11,
Even a rabbit knows that's 70 plus 7.
Multiply 7 x 12,
You got 84, and isn't that swell.
I'm gonna try 7 x 13, just for fun,
70 plus 21.
7 x 14 must be great.
Well, exactly, that's a 70 plus 28.
7 x 15, man alive
That's 70 plus 35 . . . 105!

Man, this stuff is simple—no jive.
You got it, now I gotta fly.
Excuse me folks, I'm saying good-bye.
I sure do thank you for the huckleberry pie.
Take it home, boys.

Remember Lucky Seven Sampson that's my natural-born name.
If you should ask me again, I'd have to tell you the same.
You'll wake up tomorrow, you'll be glad that I came
'Cause you'll be singin' one of the songs that I sang.
So keep a happy outlook and be good to your friend,
and maybe I'll pass this way again.
Maybe!

Bye.

TRIVIA

Dorough says he's always thought of Lucky Seven as an animated version of himself.

When Lucky Seven makes 42 "clickety clicks" on the fence (7 x 6), the wall in the background is filled with graffiti names of the people who worked on the animation: "Phunky Phil" is Phil Kimmelman, the animation director on all of the *Multiplication Rock* songs and many others.

FACTS

First Aired in 1973
Lyrics and Music by Bob Dorough
Performed by Bob Dorough
Designed by Rowland Wilson
Animation by Phil Kimmelman
    and Associates

FIGURE EIGHT

SYNOPSIS

In a one-room
schoolhouse,
a young blond girl
with purple bows
in her hair
daydreams about
skating perfect
figure eights
and staying
clear
of thin ice.
A little bundled-
up boy ignores
the warning and
springs out of the
frigid water a
blue,
chattering fright.
He's soon followed
by an octopus,
8 submarine
periscopes
(with 2 eyes
peering out
of each one),
24 fish, a speed skater
hitting
the thermometer at
32, and the tempera-
ture rising to 40.

Figure eight as double four,
Figure four as half of eight.
If you skate, you would be great
If you could make a figure 8.
That's a circle that turns 'round upon itself.

1 x 8 is 2 x 4.
    4 x 4 is 2 x 8.
        If you skate upon thin ice,
        You'd be wise if you thought twice
        Before you made another single move.

1 x 8 is 8, 2 x 8 is 16,
    3 x 8 is 24, 4 x 8 is 32,
    and 5 x 8 is 40, you know.

6 x 8 is 48, 7 x 8 is 56,
8 x 8 is 64, 9 x 8 is 72,
    and 10 x 8 is 80, that's true.

11 x 8 is 88, and 12 x 8 is 96.
Now, here's a chance to get off
On your new math tricks.
'Cause 12 x 8 is the same as
10 x 8 plus 2 x 8
80 plus 16 . . . 96

1 x 8 is 8, 2 x 8 is 16
3 x 8 is 24, 4 x 8 is 32
and 5 x 8 is 40, you know.

Figure eight as double four,
Figure four as half of eight.
If you skate, you would be great,
If you could make a figure 8.
That's a circle that turns 'round upon itself.

Place it on its side and it's a symbol meaning
Infinity . . .

TRIVIA

Many first learned about the infinity sign from this spot, the favorite of all *Multiplication Rock* tunes.

The one-room schoolhouse and the busload of kids tramping through the snow became the opening billboard for *Multiplication Rock*.

The "model" for the little blond skater was Gretchen Grace, the daughter of good friends of the Yohes.

When Dorough wrote the tune for this song, he decided the melody was far too pretty to be a *Multiplication Rock* song. But when subsequent music was written, no one liked it, so Dorough returned to the original.

Blossom Dearie had the childlike voice everyone wanted for this song. A cabaret artist, you'll recognize her distinct voice singing the melody for Calvin Klein's Eternity perfume ads.

FACTS

First Aired in 1973
Lyrics and Music by Bob Dorough
Performed by Blossom Dearie
Designed by Tom Yohe
Animation by Phil Kimmelman and Associates

NAUGHTY NUMBER NINE

SYNOPSIS

A hip take on cat-and-mouse games . . . Naughty Number Nine is a fat, orange, pool-hustling cat dressed in a purple jacket and a striped "9" tie and smoking a cigar. (And he looks like he's already used up a few of his allotted nine lives.) He uses the poor, little mouse as the cue ball and cue chalk to show the short cuts when multiplying by 9.

Ultimately, the mouse figures out how to beat Number Nine by hiding inside the "9" ball. After the cat lifts his hat, gives a cheeky grin, and exits, the mouse comes out smiling.

Number Nine will put you on the spot.
Number Nine will tie you up, oh, in a knot.
When you're tryin'
Multiplyin' by nine,
You might give it everything you've got
And still be stopped.
If you don't know some secret way you
    can check on,
You'll break your neck on
Naughty Number Nine.

Now the first thing to keep in mind
When you're multiplyin' by nine
Is that it's one less than ten.
You see nine is the same as ten minus one.
So you could multiply your number by ten,
And then subtract the number from the result,
And you'd get the same product
As if you'd multiplied by nine
And you knew it.
I mean 8 x 9 is 80 minus 8,
And 7 x 9 is 70 minus 7, and 6 x 9 is 60 minus 6.
You could use those tricks.
'Cause you must have some secret way you can beat it,
Or else you'll meet it
        With Naughty Number Nine.

    Of course it doesn't hurt
        to know the table of nines by memory.
        It goes like this:
            1 x 9 is 9, and 2 x 9 is 18.
        (Mean old Number Nine)
        3 x 9 is 27, and 4 x 9 is 36,
        5 x 9 is 45, and 6 x 9 is 54, and 7 x 9 is 63,
        8 x 9 is 72, and 9 x 9 is 81,
        and 10 x 9 is 90

Now the digit sum is always equal to nine.
I mean, if you add 2 and 7, the digits,
You get 9, the digit sum.
That's true of any product of 9.
If they don't add up, you've made a mistake.
'Cause you must have some secret way you can check it,
Or else you'll wreck it
With naughty, nasty, mean old Number Nine.

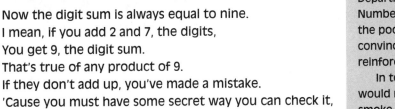

TRIVIA

The ABC Broadcast Standards and Practices (BS&P) Department objected to the cigar that Naughty Number Nine puffs throughout this spot, filling the pool hall with a toxic haze. Ultimately BS&P was convinced that the cigar was an essential prop to reinforce just how "naughty" Number Nine really was.

In today's anti-smoking climate, Number Nine would most likely have to go out to the sidewalk to smoke his stogie.

This was the first of several films that Tom Yohe and Bill Peckmann collaborated on.

FACTS

First Aired in 1973
Lyrics and Music by Bob Dorough
Performed by Grady Tate
Designed by Tom Yohe and Bill Peckmann
Animation by Phil Kimmelman and Associates

THE GOOD ELEVEN

SYNOPSIS

A winged angel takes you through the eleven-times table, but always manages to bump into the "10" along the way. We also get to see the digits in "11" play leapfrog with each other.

Good, good, good, good, the good eleven, yeah
It's almost as easy as multiplyin' by one.
Good, good, good, good eleven. (Mmm)
Yes, eleven almost makes multiplication fun.

Some people get up at a quarter till seven,
Other people lie abed till 8:45 or 9.
But I'm happy just to hang in there till 11,
'Cause eleven has always been a friend of mine.

Good, good, good, good eleven,
Never gave me any trouble till after nine.
Good, good, good, good eleven. (Mmm)
Eleven will always be a friend of mine.

Now, when you get a chance to multiply by eleven
   (eleven, Yeah!),
It's almost as easy as multiplying by one.
You don't even have to use a pencil when you use eleven,
And eleven almost makes multiplication fun.

You know why? (Yeah!)
Because you get those funny looking double-digit doogies as an answer.
Like 22, 33, 44, and 55.
66, 77, 88, and 99 is your answer
When you multiply 11 by 2, 3, 4, 5, 6, 7, 8, and 9.

Good, good, good, good, good eleven,
Never gave me any trouble till after nine.
Good, good, good, good eleven, (Mmm)
I can always get that answer easy every time.

Now 11 x 10 is the same as 10 x 11 (10 x 11),

It's 110 no matter what you do.
And 121 is the answer to 11 x 11,
And 11 x 12 is 132.
11 13's are 143, now. (That's 1-4-3)
11 14's are 154. (Dig it, it's 1-5-4)
1-6-5 and 1-7-6 are 15 and 16.
You better pick up on the pattern,
'Cause I ain't got time to tell you any more.

I've got a date with the good eleven.
She never gave me any trouble till after nine.
(Good, good, good, good)
Good, g-g-g-g-good, eleven. (Mmm)
Yes, eleven will always be a friend of mine.

TRIVIA

A new word: "doogies" (with a "g" as in germ). Here they look like people with double-digit numbers for bodies. Bob Dorough thought eleven was "good" because of the easy double-digit answers you get.

This song was omitted from the first *Schoolhouse Rock* video, which was produced by ABC, without the knowledge of the series' creators. (Yohe discovered that the cassettes had been produced when he accidentally came across a frame from "The Great American Melting Pot," accompanying a blurb about the series in *People* magazine.)

Designer Jack Sidebotham worked at McCaffrey and McCall with a lot of the characters who make brief appearances in this song, including David McCall (looking in the mirror), Newall (in the blue outfit on the bike), and Yohe (wearing a red bow tie).

FACTS

First Aired in 1973
Lyrics and Music by Bob Dorough
Performed by Bob Dorough
Designed by Jack Sidebotham
Animation by Phil Kimmelman and Associates

LITTLE TWELVETOES

SYNOPSIS

A young barefoot country boy with red hair, overalls, and a straw hat follows the twelve-toed man out of curiosity, learns the twelve-times table with the help of a celestial pinball machine, and discovers what 10 and 11 would have been called—dec, χ; and el, Σ—had we been born with six fingers on each hand.

The eeriest of the *Multiplication Rock* spots—both in its haunting music and in its notion that there are aliens out there dressed in prison attire, sporting stars on their chests, and stretching apart like Slinkies.

Now, if man
Had been born with six fingers on each hand,
He'd also have twelve toes,
Or so the theory goes . . .

Well, with twelve digits, I mean fingers,
He probably would've invented two more digits
When he invented his number system.
Then, if he'd saved the zero for the end,
He could count and multiply by 12's,
Just as easily as you and I do by 10's.

Now, if man
Had been born with six fingers on each hand,
He'd probably count: 1, 2, 3, 4, 5, 6, 7, 8, 9, dek, el, do.
Dek and el being two entirely new signs meaning 10 and 11—single digits.
And his 12, do, would've been written: one—zero.
Get it?
That'd be swell, to multiply by 12.

Hey, Little Twelvetoes, I hope you're well.
Must be some far-flung planet where you dwell.
If we were together you could be my cousin.
Down here we call 'em "a dozen."
Hey, Little Twelvetoes, please come back home . . .

Now, if man
Had been born with six fingers on each hand,
His children would have 'em too,
And when they played hide-and-go-seek, they'd count by sixes, fast.
And when they studied piano, they'd do their six-finger exercises,
And when they went to school,
They'd learn the Golden Rule,
And how to multiply by 12 easily:
Just put down the zero.
But me—I have to learn it the hard way.
Let me see now . . .

1 x 12 is 12, 2 x 12 is 24, 3 x 12 is 36, 4 x 12 is 48, 5 x 12 is 60,
6 x 12 is 72, 7 x 12 is 84, 8 x 12 is 96, 9 x 12 is 108, 10 x 12 is 120,
11 x 12 is 132, and 12 x 12 is 144.
Wow!

Hey Little Twelvetoes, I hope you're thrivin',
Some of us ten-toed folks are still survivin'.
If you help me with my 12's,
I'll help you with your 10's,
And we could all be friends.
Little Twelvetoes, please come back home.

TRIVIA

This song was also left off the first video of *SR*, and it is so difficult to sing while playing the background music that Dorough rarely performs it any more.

After Dorough wrote the song, he looked through the Manhattan phone book and found the Duodecimal Society of New York and was too busy or too shy, he says, to call them up, so he decided to dedicate the song to the Duodecimal Society of America (figuring there must be one) and to the world.

Rowland Wilson, who designed this spot and painted all of the backgrounds for the amazing celestial pinball machine, is also a well-known illustrator and a cartoonist whose work appears in *The New Yorker*.

George Newall calls this "the most underrated" of all *SR* segments. It was originally rejected when the concept was thought to be too difficult for elementary school students. But Dorothy Bloomberg, the math consultant from the Bank Street College of Education, insisted that part of effective teaching was challenging young minds.

Approval was eventually given, based on Dorothy's advice and taking into account that the segment would be repeated—so "Little Twelvetoes" joined the cast.

FACTS

First Aired in 1973
Lyrics and Music by Bob Dorough
Performed by Bob Dorough
Designed by Rowland Wilson
Animation by Phil Kimmelman and Associates

Developed in Consultation with Dr. Henry F. Beechhold

CONJUNCTION JUNCTION

SYNOPSIS

In a maze of tracks at the railroad yard, colored boxcars are linked together by our favorite train conductor, dressed in blue overalls, a puffy hat, a red bandanna, and wire-framed glasses.

The segment features two hobos—one fat and one small—frying fish, riding in a hot-air balloon, and sharing tea with the conductor. Also featured are the duck and the drake, thinking: "Conjunction Junction . . . What's your function?"; and the blonde tied up on the railroad tracks.

At the end, watch for the conductor waving from the caboose.

Conjunction Junction, what's your function?
Hookin' up words and phrases and clauses.
Conjunction Junction, how's that function?
I got three favorite cars that get most of my job done.
Conjunction Junction, what's their function?
I got And, But, and Or.
They'll get you pretty far.

And! That's an additive, like this and that
But! That's sort of the opposite, not this but that
And then there's Or, O-R,
When you have a choice like this or that.
And, But, and Or get you pretty far!

Conjunction Junction, what's your function?
Hookin' up two boxcars and makin' 'em run right.
Milk and honey, bread and butter, peas and rice,
(Hey, that's nice)
Dirty but happy, diggin' and scratchin',
Losing your shoe and a button or two,
He was poor but honest, sad but true,
Boo-hoo-hoo-hoo-hoo.

Conjunction Junction, what's your function?
Hookin' up two cars to one when you say
Somethin' like this choice:
Either now or later,
Or no choice:
Neither now nor ever.
(Hey, that's clever)
Eat this or that, grow thin or fat.
Never mind, I wouldn't do that, I'm fat enough now!

Conjunction Junction, what's your function?
Hookin' up phrases and clauses that balance like:
Out of the frying pan and into the fire.
He cut loose the sandbags, but the balloon wouldn't go
    any higher.
Let's go up to the mountains or down to the seas.
You should always say thank you, or at least say *please*!

Conjunction Junction, what's your function?
Hookin' up words and phrases and clauses
In complex sentences like:
"In the mornings, when I'm usually wide awake,
I love to take a walk through the gardens and down by
    the lake,
Where I often see a duck and a drake,
And I wonder as I walk by, just what they'd say
If they could speak
Although I know that's an absurd thought."

Conjunction Junction, what's your function?
Hookin'-up cars and makin' 'em function.
Conjunction Junction, how's that function?
I like tyin' up words and phrases and clauses.

Conjunction Junction, watch that function!
I'm gonna get you there, if you're very careful.
Conjunction Junction, what's your function?
I'm gonna get you there if you're very careful.

TRIVIA

This is by far the most recognized *Schoolhouse Rock* tune and was the first *SR* song recorded with Jack Sheldon, legendary jazz singer and Merv Griffin's former trumpet player.

Jazz singer Terry Morel was visiting the studio in L.A. the day "Conjunction Junction" was being recorded, so Dorough asked her to sing the chorus for the demo tape, and it ended up being on the actual recording. Mary Sue Berry provided the harmony.

Tom Yohe collaborated with Bill Peckmann on this classic. Yohe provided the storyboard and character sketches of the conductor, while Peckmann designed the hobos lunching at trackside and the thoughtful duck and drake.

The original concept of a railroad yard where words and phrases are hooked together came from George Newall. (But after hearing Bob Dorough's song, Newall was relieved that he hadn't tried to write it!)

"I'm Just a Bill" and "Conjunction Junction" were recorded in L.A. on the same day, so many wonder if there's a connection between these two best-known *SR* songs. Perhaps it was the fact that they shared the same band:

Bass: Leroy Vinegar	Drummer: Nick Ceroli
Guitar: Stuart Scharf	Piano / Keyboards: Dave Frishberg
Saxophone: Teddy Edwards	Trumpet: Jack Sheldon

FACTS

First Aired in 1973
Lyrics and Music by Bob Dorough
Performed by Jack Sheldon
Designed by Tom Yohe
    and Bill Peckmann
Animation by Phil Kimmelman
    and Associates

A NOUN IS A PERSON, PLACE, OR THING

SYNOPSIS

A young girl in her short, short skirt points at nouns on a screen, then jumps through it to get in on the action.

She goes to visit grandma in another state, befriends a barking dog on Hudson Street, meets her friend at the Statue of Liberty (where it snows in April!?), and shares a soda with her friend at the local drugstore.

Well, every person you can know,
And every place that you can go,
And anything that you can show,
You know they're nouns.

A noun's a special kind of word,
It's any name you ever heard,
I find it quite interesting.
A noun's a person, place, or thing.

Oh, I took a train, took a train to another state.
The flora and fauna that I saw were really great.
I saw some bandits chasin' the train.
I was wishin' I was back home again.
I took a train, took a train to another state.

Well, every person you can know (like a bandit or an engineer)
And every place that you can go (like a state or a home)
And anything that you can show (like animals and plants or a train)
You know they're nouns—you know they're nouns, oh . . .

Mrs. Jones is a lady on Hudson Street.
She sent her dog to bark at my brother and me.
We gave her dog a big fat bone,
And now he barks at Mrs. Jones.
She's a lady who lives on Hudson Street.

Well, every person you can know (Mrs. Jones, a lady, or a brother)
And every place that you can go (like a street or a corner)
And anything that you can show (like a dog or a bone)
You know they're nouns—you know they're nouns.

Oh, I took a ferry to the Statue of Liberty.
My best friend was waitin' there for me. (He took an early ferry.)
We went for a walk on the island you know,
And in the middle of summer it started to snow,
When I took a ferry to the Statue of Liberty.

Well, every person you can know (like a friend or the captain of a ship)
And every place that you can go (an island or a sea)
And anything that you can show (like a statue, a ferry, or snow)
You know they're nouns—you know they're nouns

Oh, I put a dime in the drugstore record machine.
Oldie goldies started playing if you know what I mean.
I heard Chubby Checker, he was doin' the twist
And the Beatles and the Monkees, it goes like this!
I put a dime in the drugstore record machine.

Well, every person you can know (the Beatles and the Monkees, Chubby Checker)
And every place that you can go (like a neighborhood or a store)
And anything that you can show (like a dime or a record machine)
You know they're nouns.

A noun's a special kind of word
It's any name you ever heard.
I find it quite interesting
A noun's a person, place, or thing.

A noun is a person, place, or thing.

TRIVIA

Ah, the good times. When a song in the jukebox only cost a dime
. . . Blink and you'll miss the white Chubby Checker and Newall's
Drug Store!
    It was one of
 sixteen tunes
 Lynn Ahrens
 wrote for
 Schoolhouse Rock.

FACTS

First Aired in 1973
Lyrics and Music by Lynn Ahrens
Performed by Lynn Ahrens
Designed by Jack Sidebotham
Animation by Phil Kimmelman and Associates

VERB: THAT'S WHAT'S HAPPENING

SYNOPSIS

A young boy goes to the theater to see his favorite superhero movie, *Verb*. He's *bold* and steals a seat up in the front row. Then he pretends the theater is full of pirates and wild animals. He imagines himself climbing up a snowy peak only to be bumped off by a mountain goat and saved by Verb.

Features superhero Verb being struck by lightning turning "to be" into "not to be"; then it rains and "I am" becomes "I am wet."

When the movie is over, the boy rushes home to his mom, and the final verb is "to love."

I get my thing in action (Verb!)
To be, to see, to feel, to live (Verb!)
That's what's happenin'

I put my heart in action (Verb!)
To run, to go, to get, to give (Verb!)
(You're what's happenin')

That's where I find satisfaction, yeah! (Yeah!)
To search, to find, to have, to hold.
(Verb! To be bold)
When I use my imagination (Verb!)
I think, I plot, I plan, I dream
Turning in towards creation (Verb!)
I make, I write, I dance, I sing
When I'm feeling really active (Verb!)
I run, I ride, I swim, I fly!
Other times when life is easy
(Oh!) I rest, I sleep, I sit, I lie.

(Verb! That's what happenin')
I can take a noun and bend it,
Give me a noun—
(Bat, boat, rake, and plow)
Make it a verb and really send it!
(Show me how)
Oh, I don't know my own power. (Verb!)

A few frames from Tom Yohe's rough storyboard.

(MUSICAL INTRO) I GET MY THING IN ACTION. **VERB!**

TO BE ... TO SEE ... TO FEEL ... TO LIVE ...

I get my thing in action (Verb!)
In being, (Verb!) In doing, (Verb!)
In saying
A verb expresses action, being, or state of being.
A verb makes a statement.
Yeah, a verb tells it like it is!

(Verb! That's what's happenin'.)
I can tell you when it's happenin',
(Past, present, future tense)
Ooh! Tell you more about what's happenin',
(Say it so it makes some sense)
I can tell you who is happenin'!
(Verb, you're so intense)
Every sentence has a subject.
(Noun, person, place, or thing)
Find that subject: Where's the action?
(Verb can make a subject sing.)
Take the subject: What is it? (What!)
What's done to it? (What!)
What does it say?
(Verb, you're what's happenin')

I can question, like: What is it?
(Verb, you're so demanding.)
I can order like: Go get it!
(Verb, you're so commanding.)
When I hit I need an object
(Verb, hit! Hit the ball!)
When I see, I see the object
(Do you see that furthest wall?)

If you can see it there, put the ball over the fence, man!
Go ahead. Yeah, all right.
What?! He hit it. It's going, it's going, it's gone!
(What?!)

I get my thing in action.
(Verb, that's what happenin')
To work, (Verb!)
To play, (Verb!)
To live, (Verb!)
To love . . . (Verb! . . .)

TRIVIA

Dave Frishberg ("I'm Just a Bill") originally wrote a thought-provoking song for verbs called "A World Without Verbs," based on the idea that without verbs, nothing would happen. But the idea wasn't a hit with everyone, so Bob Dorough came up with a more action-oriented tune.

This was another Yohe/Peckmann collaboration, with Yohe drawing the storyboard and Peckmann providing the character designs and doing the animation layouts.

The late Zachary Sanders sang two *SR* songs: "Verb" and "Electricity."

FACTS

First Aired in 1974
Lyrics and Music by Bob Dorough
Performed by Zachary Sanders
Designed by Tom Yohe and Bill Peckmann
Animation by Phil Kimmelman and Associates

LOLLY, LOLLY, LOLLY, GET YOUR ADVERBS HERE

SYNOPSIS

Lolly's, Inc., is a quiet little adverb store until Lolly III (zipping around on roller skates) gets the brilliant idea to call the "TV Mobile Unit" to do a story/commercial on the establishment. Soon people from miles around are crowding the store looking to buy adverbs and transform their adjectives.

(Mmm . . . Mmm . . . Mmm)
Ready Pop? Yup.
Ready son? Uh-huh.
Let's go!
Let's go!
One! Two! . . .

Lolly, Lolly, Lolly, get your adverbs here.
Lolly, Lolly, Lolly, got some adverbs here.
Come on down to Lolly's, get the
    adverbs here
You're going to need
If you write or read,
Or even think about it.

Lolly, Lolly, Lolly, get your adverbs here.
Got a lot of lolly, jolly adverbs here.
Anything you need and we can make it absolutely clear . . .

An adverb is a word
(That's all it is! And there's a lot of them)
That modifies a verb,
(Sometimes a verb and sometimes)
It modifies an adjective, or else another adverb
And so you see that it's positively, very, very necessary.

Lolly, Lolly, Lolly, get your adverbs here.
Father, son, and Lolly selling adverbs here.
Got a lot of adverbs, and we make it clear,
So come to Lolly! (Lolly, Lolly, Lolly)

Hello folks, this is Lolly, Sr., saying we have every adverb in the book, so come on down and look.

Hello folks, Lolly, Jr., here. Suppose your house needs painting—how are you going to paint it? That's where the adverb comes in. We can also give you a special intensifier so you can paint it very neatly or rather sloppily.

Hi! Suppose you're going nut gathering; your buddy wants to know where and when. Use an adverb and tell him!

Get your adverbs!

Use it with an adjective, it says much more,
Anything described can be described some more.
Anything you'd ever need is in the store,
And so you choose very carefully every word you use.

Use it with a verb, it tells us how you did,
Where it happened, where you're going, where you've been.
Use it with another adverb—that's the end,
And even more . . .

How, where, or when,
Condition or reason,
These questions are answered
When you use an adverb.

Come and get it!

Lolly, Lolly, Lolly, get your adverbs here.
Quickly, quickly, quickly, get those adverbs here.
Slowly, surely, really learn your adverbs here.
You're going to need 'em if you read 'em,
If you write or talk or think about 'em . . . Lolly! (Lolly, Lolly, Lolly)

ANNOUNCER: If it's an adverb, we have it at Lolly's. Bring along your old adjectives,
    too—like slow, soft, and sure. We'll fit 'em out with our L-Y
    attachment and make perfectly good adverbs out of them!

(Get your adverbs here!)

Lots of good tricks at Lolly's so come on down.

(Lolly, Lolly, Lolly)

Adverbs deal with manner, place, time,
(Lolly, Lolly, Lolly)
Condition, reason,
(Father, son, and Lolly)
Comparison, contrast
(Lolly, Lolly, Lolly)
Enrich your language with adverbs!
(Lolly, Lolly, Lolly)
Besides they're absolutely free!
(Lolly, Lolly, Lolly)
At your service.

Indubitably.

TRIVIA

Check out the pickled adverbs,
frozen adverbs, and six-packs of adverbs . . .
not to mention the stacks of "LY" endings.
    Bob Dorough is the voice of all three
generations of Lollys. His voice was speeded
up to vary the pitch.

FACTS

First Aired in 1974
Lyrics and Music by Bob Dorough
Performed by Bob Dorough
Designed by Jack Sidebotham
Animation by Phil Kimmelman and Associates

UNPACK YOUR ADJECTIVES

SYNOPSIS

A girl and her pet turtle unpack adjectives from an enormous backpack to describe their camping trip. As they walk through the woods, they label everything with adjective signs. And when they run into the bear, he eats the adjective signs they pull out to describe him.

Watch when they emerge from their tent yawning, collapse the tent, and after a few pats it magically turns back into the backpack.

Also features the funny scene when, in describing tall vs. small, the tall girl stomps on the small boy when he won't stop giggling at how big she is.

Got home from camping last spring.
Saw people, places, and things.
We barely had arrived,
Friends asked us to describe
The people, places, and every last thing.
So we unpacked our adjectives.

I unpacked "frustrating" first.
Reached in and found the word "worst."
Then I picked "soggy" and
Next I picked "foggy" and
Then I was ready to tell them my tale,
'Cause I'd unpacked my adjectives.

Adjectives are words you use to really describe things.
Handy words to carry around.
Days are sunny, or they're rainy.
Boys are dumb or else they're brainy.
Adjectives can show you which way.

Adjectives are often used to help us compare things,
To say how thin, how fat, how short, how tall.
Girls who're tall get taller.
Boys who're small get smaller,
Till one is the tallest and the other's the smallest of all.
We hiked along without care.
Then we ran into a bear!
He was a hairy bear!
He was a scary bear!
We beat a hasty retreat from his lair,
And described him with adjectives!

TURTLE: Wow! Boy, that was one big, ugly bear!

You can make even adjectives out of the other parts of speech like verbs and nouns. All you have to do is tack on an ending like "-ic" or "-ish" or "-ary." For example: This boy can grow up to be a huge man, but still have a boyish face. Boy is a noun, but the ending "-ish" makes it an adjective, boyish, that describes the huge man's face. Get it?

Next time you go on a trip,
Remember this little tip:
The minute you get back,
They'll ask you this and that.
You can describe people, places, and things.
Simply unpack your adjectives.
You can do it with adjectives.
Tell 'em about it with adjectives.
You can shout it with adjectives.

TRIVIA

This was the first of several songs that George Newall (a music major turned advertising copywriter) contributed to the series.

The "demo" was originally sung by Bob Dorough, but it was then decided to record the final track with Blossom Dearie ("Figure Eight"). So the camper became a little girl (Newall still marvels that Dearie actually recorded something he wrote), and Dorough was the voice of the turtle.

FACTS

First Aired in 1975
Lyrics and Music by George Newall
Performed by Blossom Dearie
Designed by Tom Yohe
Animation by Phil Kimmelman
    and Associates

HE

RUFUS XAVIER SARSAPARILLA

SYNOPSIS

Three friends with complicated names and rather exotic, color-coordinated pets illustrate the value of pronouns whether in the jungle or on a bus.

On a pogo stick, Rufus and his kangaroo bounce along in orange; Rafaella wears springs on her feet to keep up with her matching pink aardvark; and Albert (our narrator), in his yellow wardrobe, is the perfect match for his yellow rhino.

Now, I have a friend named Rufus Xavier Sarsaparilla,
And I could say that Rufus found a kangaroo
That followed Rufus home
And now that kangaroo belongs
To Rufus Xavier Sarsaparilla.

RUFUS XAVIER SARSAPARILLA

Whew! I could say that,
    but I don't have to,
'Cause I've got pronouns,
I can say, "HE found a kangaroo that
    followed HIM home and now IT is HIS"

You see, (uh) HE, HIM, and HIS
    are pronouns,
Replacing the noun,
Rufus Xavier Sarsaparilla,
A very proper noun.
And IT is a pronoun, replacing the noun, kangaroo! (How common!)

Now Rufus has a sister named Rafaella Gabriela Sarsaparilla.
If she found a kangaroo I'd say to you:
"SHE found a kangaroo that followed HER home, and now it is HERS."
But I can't say that . . .

PRONOUN

            'Cause SHE found an aardvark
            That fell in love with HER, and THEY're so happy.

And my name's Albert Andreas Armadillo.
(No relation to the Sarsaparillas.)
Because of pronouns, I can say:
"I wish SHE would find a rhinoceros for ME and WE'd be happy."

You see, a pronoun was made to take the place of a noun,
'Cause saying all those nouns over and over
Can really wear you down!

Now I could tell you Rafaella Gabriela and Rufus Xavier Sarsaparilla and Albert Andreas Armadillo found an aardvark,
a kangaroo, and a rhinoceros. And now that aardvark and that kangaroo and that rhinoceros belong respectively to Rafaella Gabriela Sarsaparilla and Rufus Xavier Sarsaparilla and Albert Andreas Armadillo!

Whew! Because of pronouns I can say, in this way:
"WE found THEM and THEY found US and now THEY are OURS
    and WE're so happy."

Thank you, pronouns!

You see a pronoun was made to take the place of a noun,
'Cause saying all those nouns over and over
Can really wear you down.

Sometimes, when we take 'em all on the bus
People really raise a fuss.
They start shouting out a lot o' pronouns at us, like
"WHO brought that rhinoceros on this bus?" and
"WHAT made that horrible noise?"and
"WHICH one of them is getting off first?"

WHO, WHAT, and WHICH are special pronouns that can ask a question
In a sentence when you do not know the name of the noun,
But I know:
I have MINE, and SHE has HERS,
HE has HIS. Do YOU have YOURS?
THEY love US, and WE love THEM,
WHAT's OURS is THEIRS—
That's how it is with friends,
And pronouns, you are really friends, yeah!

'Cause saying all those nouns over and over
Can really wear you down.

TRIVIA

Lew Gifford's bold designs and bright colors make this a graphic delight. Enjoy watching the "elasticity" of the bus when the animals crowd aboard.

Kathy Mandry was a copywriter at McCaffrey and McCall when she wrote the lyrics to this tune. She was also a children's book author, and thus a natural to try her hand at educational song writing.

FACTS

First Aired in 1977
Music and Lyrics by Kathy Mandry and Bob Dorough
Performed by Jack Sheldon
Designed by Paul Kim and Lew Gifford
Animation by Kim and Gifford Productions

INTERJECTIONS!

(Cough - cough - cough)

When Reginald was home with flu, uh-huh-huh,
The doctor knew just what to do-hoo.
He cured the infection
With one small injection
While Reginald uttered some interjections . . .

Hey! That smarts!
Ouch! That hurts!
Yow! That's not fair givin' a guy a shot down there!
Interjections (Hey!) show excitement (Yow!) or emotion (Ouch!).
They're generally set apart from a sentence by an exclamation point
Or by a comma when the feeling's not as strong.

Though Geraldine played hard to get, uh-huh-huh
Geraldo knew he'd woo her ye-het
He showed his affection
Despite her objections
And Geraldine hollered some interjections . . .

Well! You've got some nerve!
Oh! I've never been so insulted in all my life.
Hey! You're kinda cute!

Interjections (Well!) show excitement (Oh!)
    or emotion (Hey!).
They're generally set apart from a sentence
    by an exclamation point,
Or by a comma when the feeling's not as strong.

SYNOPSIS

A series of hilarious scenes depict the different types of interjections: Hurray! —cheerleading squad; Aw!—pitcher on the mound when it starts to rain; Eeek!—snake scared by a girl; Rats!—go-cart racer whose wheel falls off; Wow!—teen with A+ report card; Hey!—little girl learning to ride a two-wheeler.

So when you're happy (Hurray!) or sad (Aw!)
Or frightened (Eeek!) or mad (Rats!)
Or excited (Wow!) or glad (Hey!)
An interjection starts a sentence right.

The game was tied at seven all, uh-huh-huh,
When Franklin found he had the ba-hall.
He made a connection
In the other direction,
The crowd started shoutin' out interjections . . .

Aw! You threw the wrong way!
Darn! You just lost the game!
Hurray! I'm for the other team!

Interjections (Aw!) show excitement (Darn!) or emotion (Hurray!).
They're generally set apart from a sentence by an exclamation point,
Or by a comma when the feeling's not as strong.

So when you're happy (Hurray!) or sad (Aw!)
Or frightened (Eeek!) or mad (Rats!)
Or excited (Wow!) or glad (Hey!)
An interjection starts a sentence right.

Interjections (Hey!) show excitement (Hey!) or emotion (Hey!).
They're generally set apart from a sentence by an exclamation point,
Or by a comma when the feeling's not as strong.

Interjections show excitement or emotion,
Hallelujah, hallelujah, hallelujah, YEA!

GIRL: Darn! That's the end!

Darn! That's The End!

TRIVIA

Our favorite "Darn! That's the End!" girl is the voice of Tom Yohe's daughter, Lauren, who was then just six years old. Tom Yohe, Jr.—now an advertising art director like his father—provided the voice for Reginald. And Lynn Ahrens added the "Wow!" for the girl with the A+.

Co-producer Radford Stone is the voice of the outraged fan reacting to quarterback Franklin's confusion: "Aw! You threw the wrong way!" It only took Stone six takes.

This was Lynn Ahrens' favorite segment in terms of the animation.

The song borrows its classical finale from Handel's *Messiah*, "The Hallelujah Chorus."

FACTS

First Aired in 1974
Lyrics and Music by Lynn Ahrens
Performed by Essra Mohawk
Designed by Tom Yohe
Animation by Phil Kimmelman
    and Associates

Developed in Consultation with Professor John A. Garraty

NO MORE KINGS

Rockin' and rollin', splishin' and a-splashin',
Over the horizon, what can it be?

The pilgrims sailed the sea
To find a place to call their own.
In their ship, *Mayflower*,
They hoped to find a better home.
They finally knocked
On Plymouth Rock
And someone said, "We're there."
It may not look like home
But at this point I don't care.

Oh, they were missing Mother England,
They swore their loyalty until the very end.
Anything you say, King,
It's OK, King,
You know it's kinda scary on your own.
Gonna build a new land
The way we planned.
Could you help us run it till it's grown?

They planted corn, you know
They built their houses one by one,
And bit by bit they worked
Until the colonies were done.
They looked around,
Yeah, up and down,
And someone said, "Hurray!"
If the king could only see us now
He would be proud of us today.

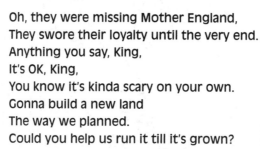

They knew that now they'd run their own land,
But George the Third still vowed
He'd rule them to the end.
Anything I say, do it my way now.

Anything I say, do it my way.
Don't you get to feeling independent
'Cause I'm gonna force you to obey.

He taxed their property,
He didn't give them any choice,
And back in England
He didn't give them any voice.
(That's called taxation without representation,
And it's not fair!)
But when the Colonies complained
The king said: "I don't care!"

He even has the nerve
To tax our cup of tea.
To put it kindly, King,
We really don't agree.

Gonna show you how we feel.
We're gonna dump this tea
And turn this harbor into
The biggest cup of tea in history!

They wanted no more Mother England.
They knew the time had come
For them to take command.
It's very clear you're being unfair, King,
No matter what you say, we won't obey.
Gonna hold a revolution now, King,
And we're gonna run it all our way
With no more kings . . .

We're gonna elect a president! (No more kings)
He's gonna do what the people want! (No more kings)
We're gonna run things our way! (No more kings)
Nobody's gonna tell us what to do!

Rockin' and rollin', splishin' and a-splashing,
Over the horizon, what can it be?
Looks like it's going to be a free country.

(Applause)

TRIVIA

America Rock (also called *History Rock* by some)
was created to coincide with the Bicentennial
celebration in 1976.

Tom Yohe provided King George's gleeful cackle
as he counts his money and rubs his hands together.

FACTS

First Aired in 1975
Lyrics and Music by Lynn Ahrens
Performed by Lynn Ahrens
Designed by Paul Kim/Lew Gifford
Animation by Kim and Gifford Productions

THE SHOT HEARD 'ROUND THE WORLD

SYNOPSIS

The rebels defeat the British in this animated version of the Revolutionary War, from Paul Revere's famous ride and the first battles at Lexington and Concord, through Valley Forge, Bunker Hill, and Washington's crossing of the Delaware . . . and finally, to the British surrender at Yorktown. A referee declares the rebels to be the winners.

"The British are coming! The British are coming!"

Now, the ride of Paul Revere
Set the nation on its ear,
And the shot at Lexington heard
    'round the world,
When the British fired in the early dawn
The War of Independence had begun,
The die was cast, the rebel flag unfurled.

And on to Concord marched the foe
To seize the arsenal there you know,
Waking folks and searching all around
Till our militia stopped them in their tracks,
At the old North Bridge we turned them back
And chased those redcoats back to Boston town.

And the shot heard 'round the world
Was the start of the Revolution.
The Minute Men were ready, on the move.
Take your powder, and take your gun.
Report to General Washington.
Hurry men, there's not an hour to lose!

Now, at famous Bunker Hill,
Even though we lost, it was quite a thrill,
The rebel Colonel Prescott proved he was wise;
Outnumbered and low on ammunition
As the British stormed his position
He said, "Hold your fire till you see the whites of their eyes!"

Though the next few years were rough,
General Washington's men proved they were tough,
Those hungry, ragged boys would not be beat.
One night they crossed the Delaware,
Surprised the Hessians in their lair,
And at Valley Forge they just bundled up their feet!

Now the shot heard 'round the world
Was the start of the Revolution.
The Minute Men were ready, on the move.
Take your blanket, and take your son.
Report to General Washington.
We've got our rights and now it's time to prove.

Well, they showed such determination
That they won the admiration
Of countries across the sea like France and Spain,
Who loaned the colonies ships and guns
And put the British on the run
And the Continental Army on its feet again.

And though they lost some battles too,
The Americans swore they'd see it through,
Their raiding parties kept up, hit and run.
At Yorktown the British could not retreat,
Bottled up by Washington and the French Fleet,
Cornwallis surrendered and finally we had won!

From the shot heard 'round the world
To the end of the Revolution
The continental rabble took the day
And the father of our country
Beat the British there at Yorktown
And brought freedom to you and me and the U.S.A.!

God Bless America, Let Freedom Ring!

TRIVIA

Look for the Weeble rebel who wobbles but
bounces back to attack the redcoats, and the
naked lady in Southern California.

FACTS

First Aired in 1976
Lyrics and Music by Bob Dorough
Performed by Bob Dorough
Designed by Jack Sidebotham
Animation by Kim and Gifford Productions

THE PREAMBLE

Establish Justice

SYNOPSIS

A brief history of the Constitution, it depicts jurors in the courtroom establishing justice, a baseball umpire insuring domestic tranquility, and voters securing the blessings of liberty. Features a little girl who keeps trying to cast her vote and the Constitution being stamped at the bottom with "OK"and "Right On!"

Hey, do you know about the U.S.A.?
Do you know about the government?
Can you tell me about the Constitution?
Hey, learn about the U.S.A.

In 1787 I'm told
Our founding fathers did agree
To write a list of principles
For keepin' people free.

The U.S.A. was just startin' out.
A whole brand-new country.
And so our people spelled it out
The things that we should be.

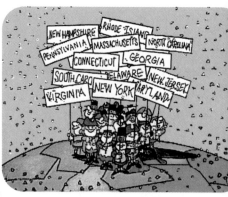

And they put those principles down on paper and called it the Constitution, and it's been helping us run our country ever since then. The first part of the Constitution is called the preamble and tells what those founding fathers set out to do.

We the people
In order to form a more perfect union,
Establish justice, insure domestic tranquility,
Provide for the common defense,
Promote the general welfare and
Secure the blessings of liberty
To ourselves and our posterity
Do ordain and establish this Constitution
    for the United States of America.

In 1787 I'm told
Our founding fathers all sat down
And wrote a list of principles
That's known the world around.

The U.S.A. was just starting out
A whole brand-new country.
And so our people spelled it out
They wanted a land of liberty.
And the preamble goes like this:

We the people
In order to form a more perfect union,
Establish justice, insure domestic tranquility,
Provide for the common defense,
Promote the general welfare and
Secure the blessings of liberty
To ourselves and our posterity,
Do ordain and establish this Constitution
     for the United States of America.

For the United States of America . . .

TRIVIA

Lynn Ahrens' first job out of college was at McCaffrey and McCall. She often brought her guitar to work to play during lunchtime. When George Newall and Tom Yohe got wind of this, they asked her if she wanted to write an *SR* song. She agreed to give it a try and went off to write "The Preamble." (Yes, she had to look up the words . . .)

She remembers it clearly because everything seemed to be going right: she had just been made a copywriter; sold a song; and was on her way to England with her future husband. It would also be her first time in front of the microphone.

This was the winner for most-hummed-during-history-tests. In New Canaan, Connecticut, an American history high school teacher was startled to hear musical murmuring during the exam. Her students were singing "The Preamble," and they all passed.

A young Canadian-born woman tracked down Newall and Yohe to tell them she wouldn't have passed her U.S. citizenship test without the help of this song.

Check out the names in the voting booth . . . Tom Yohe, Sal Faillace, George Newall, Rad Stone, George Cannata, Hal Hoffer, Lyn (spelled wrong!) Ahrens, and her husband Niel (also spelled wrong!) Costa.

You may notice that the animator, Sal Faillace, had the final say in the election, voting for himself and animation director George Cannata.

Future students should note that the founding fathers actually began the preamble: "We the people of the United States . . ."

FACTS

First Aired in 1976
Lyrics and Music by Lynn Ahrens
Performed by Lynn Ahrens
Designed by Tom Yohe
    and George Cannata
Animation by George Cannata

FIREWORKS

SYNOPSIS

We learn about the Declaration of Independence from the headlines of *The Daily Bugle* and picket signs that state THE KING STINKS! in this celebratory song.

Ooh, there's gonna be fireworks (fireworks!)
On the Fourth of July (red, white and blue!)
Red, white, and blue fireworks
Like diamonds in the sky (diamonds in the sky!)
We're gonna shoot the entire works on fireworks
That really show, oh yeah,
We declared our liberty two hundred years ago.

Yeah!

In 1776 (fireworks!)
There were fireworks too (red, white, and blue!)
The original colonists,
    You know their tempers blew (They really blew!)
    Like Thomas Paine once wrote:
    It's only common sense (only common sense)
    That if a government won't give you your basic rights
    You better get another government.

    And though some people tried to fight it,
    Well, a committee was formed to write it:
    Benjamin Franklin, Philip Livingston,
    John Adams, Roger Sherman, Thomas Jefferson,
    They got it done, (Oh yes they did!)
The Declaration, uh-huh-huh,
The Declaration of Independence (Oh yeah!)
In 1776 (Right on!)
The Continental Congress said that we were free (We're free!)
Said we had the right of life and liberty,
 . . . And the pursuit of happiness!

Ooh, when England heard the news (Kerpow!),
They blew their stack (They really blew their cool!),
But the colonies lit the fuse,
There'd be no turning back (no turning back!).
They'd had enough of injustice now
But even if it really hurts, oh yeah,
If you don't give us our freedom now
You're gonna see some fireworks!

And on the Fourth of July they signed it
And fifty-six names underlined it,
And now to honor those first thirteen states,
We turn the sky into a birthday cake.
They got it done (Oh yes they did!)
The Declaration, uh-huh-huh,
The Declaration of Independence (Oh yeah!)
In 1776 (Right on!)
The Continental Congress said that we were free (We're free!)
Said we had the right of life and liberty,
. . . And the pursuit of happiness!

We hold these truths to be self evident,
That all men are created equal
And that they are endowed by their creator
With certain unalienable rights.
That among these are life, liberty, and the pursuit
    of happiness,

And if there's one thing that makes me happy,
Then you know that it's (ooh!)
There's gonna be fireworks!

TRIVIA

Remember the comical, but now politically incorrect, scene of a man chasing a woman back and forth across the screen to depict "the pursuit of happiness"?

The little girl reciting "That all men are created equal" is co-producer Radford Stone's daughter Charlotte, then ten years old. Her brother Ian, age twelve, is the Boy Scout who follows with: "And that they are endowed by their Creator."

The passage concludes with the "certain *una*lienable rights," a tongue twister that gave Tom Yohe's daughter, Suzanne, some problems before she finally nailed it. Sort of.

FACTS

First Aired in 1977
Lyrics and Music
    by Lynn Ahrens
Performed by Grady Tate
Designed by Tom Yohe
Animation by Phil Kimmelman
    and Associates

ELBOW ROOM

SYNOPSIS

The Louisiana Purchase, Manifest Destiny, land runs, and westward expansion set to music with lots of chickenlike elbow dancing. Lewis and Clark take along a CARE package, and OREGON OR BUST sweeps the nation. It ignores the plight of Native Americans, but predicts lunar colonization!

One thing you will discover
When you get next to one another
Is everybody needs some elbow room, elbow room.

It's nice when you're kinda cozy, but
Not when you're tangled nose
   to nosey, oh,
Everybody needs some elbow, needs
   a little elbow room.

That's how it was in the early days
   of the U.S.A.,
The people kept coming to settle though
The east was the only place there
   was to go.

The President was Thomas Jefferson
He made a deal with Napoleon.
How'd you like to sell a mile or two, (or three, or a hundred or a thousand?)
And so, in 1803 the Louisiana Territory was sold to us
Without a fuss
And gave us lots of elbow room,

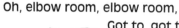

   Oh, elbow room, elbow room,
      Got to, got to get us some elbow room.
      It's the West or bust,
      In God we trust.
        There's a new land out there . . .
        Lewis and Clark volunteered to go,
        Good-bye, good luck, wear your overcoat!
      They prepared for good times and for bad (and for bad),
      They hired Sacajawea to be their guide.
     She led them all across the countryside.
     Reached the coast
     And found the most
    Elbow room we've ever had.

The way was opened up for folks with bravery.
There were plenty of fights
To win land rights,
But the West was meant to be;
It was our Manifest Destiny!

The trappers, traders, and the peddlers,
The politicians and the settlers,
They got there by any way they could (any way they could).
The Gold Rush trampled down the wilderness,
The railroads spread across from East to West,
And soon the rest was opened up for—opened up for good.

And now we jet from East to West.
Good-bye New York, hello L.A.,
But it took those early folks to open up the way.

Now we've got a lot of room to be
Growing from sea to shining sea.
Guess that we have got our elbow room (elbow room)
But if there should ever come a time
When we're crowded up together, I'm
Sure we'll find some elbow room . . . up on the moon!

Oh, elbow room, elbow room.
Got to, got to get us some elbow room.
It's the moon or bust,
In God we trust.
There's a new land up there!

TRIVIA

Yohe and Newall agree that in today's social climate, "Manifest Destiny" wouldn't have shown up in the song.

One of the designers, Paul Frahm, was an art director at the advertising agency Young & Rubicam when he storyboarded "Elbow Room." Other SR designers who were also Y&R art directors include Bob Eggers ("The Four-Legged Zoo"), Rowland B. Wilson ("Lucky Seven Sampson" and "Little Twelvetoes"), Tom Yohe, and Jack Sidebotham ("A Noun Is a Person, Place, or Thing," "Interplanet Janet," et al.), who hired Yohe at Y&R in 1960.

Bob Dorough is the voice of Thomas Jefferson.

FACTS

First Aired in 1976
Lyrics and Music by
    Lynn Ahrens
Performed by
    Sue Manchester
Designed by
    Paul Frahm and
    Lew Gifford
Animation by
    Kim and Gifford
    Productions

THE GREAT AMERICAN MELTING POT

SYNOPSIS

Kids of all backgrounds jump into one big swimming pool–like pot (shaped like the U.S.A.) as a girl looks through her family album in this sepia-tone depiction of America's conglomeration of ethnicity.

It's revealed that the book the Statue of Liberty holds is actually a cookbook, with the recipe for "Great American Melting Pot" appearing after Hungarian Goulash and Irish Stew.

My grandmother came from Russia
A satchel on her knee,
My grandfather had his father's cap
He brought from Italy.
They'd heard about a country
Where life might let them win,
They paid the fare to America
And there they melted in.

Lovely Lady Liberty
With her book of recipes
And the finest one she's got
Is the great American melting pot
The great American melting pot.

America was founded by the English,
But also by the Germans, Dutch, and French.
The principle still sticks;
Our heritage is mixed.
So any kid could be the president.

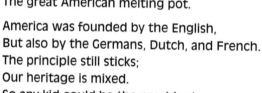

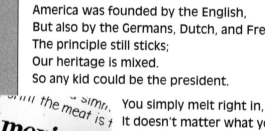

Great American Melting Pot ★

Ingredients:

Armenians, Africans, English, Dutch, Italians, Chinese, Poles, Irish, Germa Puerto Ricans, Portuguese, Spaniard Swedes, Norwegians, Russians Greeks, Cubans, Mexicans Japanese, Koreans

...the meat is...

You simply melt right in,
It doesn't matter what your skin,
It doesn't matter where you're from,
Or your religion, you jump right in
To the great American melting pot
The great American melting pot.
Ooh, what a stew, red, white, and blue.

America was the New World
And Europe was the Old.
America was the land of hope,
Or so the legend told.
On steamboats by the millions,
In search of honest pay,
Those nineteenth century immigrants sailed
To reach the U.S.A.

Lovely Lady Liberty
With her book of recipes
And the finest one she's got
Is the great American melting pot
The great American melting pot.
What good ingredients,
Liberty and immigrants.

They brought the country's customs,
Their language and their ways.
They filled the factories, tilled the soil,
Helped build the U.S.A.
Go on and ask your grandma,
Hear what she has to tell
How great to be American
And something else as well.

Lovely Lady Liberty
With her book of recipes
And the finest one she's got
Is the great American melting pot
The great American melting pot.

The great American melting pot.
The great American melting pot.

TRIVIA

Notice the factory smokestack that says "Yohe" . . . It was used as part of Radio City Music Hall's "America" Spectacular, along with other *America Rock* animation, as a backdrop for the Rockettes. "It was really embarrassing to see my name projected about four stories tall," says Yohe.

FACTS

First Aired in 1977
Lyrics and Music by Lynn Ahrens
Performed by Lori Lieberman
Designed by Tom Yohe
Animation by Kim and Gifford Productions

MOTHER NECESSITY

SYNOPSIS

Profiles of America's early inventors, including Eli Whitney, Thomas Edison, Elias Howe, Alexander Graham Bell, and Orville and Wilbur Wright. It claims they were inspired by their own mothers' dilemmas, portrayed in this *Schoolhouse Rock* episode by Mother Necessity, because "necessity is the mother of invention."

Mother Necessity
With her good intentions,
Where would this country be
Without her inventions?

Oh, things were rotten in the land of cotton
Until Whitney made the cotton gin.
Now old times there will soon be forgotten
For it did the work of a hundred men.

Mother Necessity, where would we be?

Mother Edison worked late each night.
It went well until the fading light.
Little Thomas Alva Edison said, "I'll grow up to be
A great inventor and I'll make a lamp to help my mommy see,
Wowee! What an excellent application of electricity!"
He worked hard and pulled the switch.
He was smart and very rich.

Mother Necessity, help us to see.

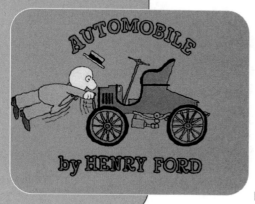

Now, the mother of Samuel Morse
Always sent the lad out on a horse.
"Take a message to Ms. Peavy on the far side of the pike;
Spread the word about the quilting bee next Saturday night!"
Little Samuel started thinking of a way to send a message,
Though he'd never met a horse he didn't like. Uh!

Mother Necessity!

Elias, can you help me with my sewing?
Mother dear, I'll fulfill your fondest wishes.

Elias, how?
This machine I've made will keep your sewing really flowing.
In fact, we'll keep the whole nation in stitches. Ah!

Mother Necessity, where would we be?

Ring me on the Alexander Graham Bell.
Thank you Alexander for the phone.
I'd never get a date, I'd never get a job
Unless I had a telephone.

Mother Necessity!

"Orville, Wilbur, go outside this minute,
And there continue with your silly playing!
Take these plans and take those blueprints.
Take that funny looking thing,
Take that wheel, take that wing,
I can't hear a thing that Mrs. Johnson's saying.
Orville! Wilbur! Come back, boys! Orville! Wilbur!"

Mother Necessity, where would we be?

When Robert Fulton made the steamboat go,
When Marconi gave us wireless radio,
When Henry Ford cranked up his first automo,
When Samuel Slater showed us how the factories go,
And all the iron and oil and coal and steel and Yankee don't
    you know,
They made this country really grow, grow, grow, grow,
With Mother Necessity and where would we be
Without the inventions of your progeny?

TRIVIA

Because the song required four singers, all of whom worked in different locations, this song was recorded in different bits on both coasts and then mixed together in New York.

FACTS

First Aired in 1977
Lyrics and Music by Bob Dorough
Performed by Bob Dorough, Blossom Dearie, Essra Mohawk, and Jack Sheldon
Designed by Jack Sidebotham
Animation by Kim and Gifford Productions

SUFFERIN' TILL SUFFRAGE

SYNOPSIS

In this empowering song, a young woman with her hair in rollers turns into a star-spangled superwoman and takes us through the history of women being unable to vote and their difficult battle to secure this basic right . . . set against a backdrop of vintage photos.

Now you have heard of Women's Rights,
And how we've tried to reach new heights.
If we're "all created equal" . . .
That's us too!

(Yeah!)

But you will proba . . . bly not recall
That it's not been too . . . too long at all.
Since we even had the right to
Cast a vote.

(Well!)

Well, sure, some men bowed down
    and called us "Mrs." (Yeah!)
Let us hang the wash out and wash the dishes, (Huh!)
But when the time rolled around to elect a president . . .

What did they say, Sister, (What did they say?)

They said, uh, "See ya later, alligator,
And don't forget my . . . my mashed potatoes
'Cause I'm going downtown to cast
    my vote for president."

Oh, we were suffering until suffrage,
Not a woman here could vote,
    no matter what age,
Then the nineteenth amendment struck
    down that restrictive rule. (Oh yeah!)

And now we pull down on the lever,
Cast our ballots and we endeavor
To improve our country, state, county,
    town, and school.

(Tell 'em 'bout it!)

Those pilgrim women who . . .
who braved the boat
Could cook the turkey, but they . . .
they could not vote.
Even Betsy Ross who sewed the flag was left behind that first election day.

(What a shame, Sisters!)

Then Susan B. Anthony (Yeah!) and Julia Howe,
(Lucretia!) Lucretia Mott, (and others!) they showed us how;
They carried signs and marched in lines
Until at long last the law was passed.

Oh, we were suffering until suffrage,
Not a woman here could vote, no matter what age,
Then the nineteenth amendment struck down that restrictive rule (Oh yeah!)

And now we pull down on the lever,
Cast our ballots and we endeavor
To improve our country, state, county, town, and school. (Right on! Right on!)

Yes, the nineteenth amendment
Struck down that restrictive rule. (Right on! Right on!)

Yes, the nineteenth amendment
Struck down that restrictive rule.
Yeah Yeah
Yeah Yeah
Right on!
We got it now!

Since 1920 . . .
Sisters, unite!
Vote on!

TRIVIA

The bell-bottoms and lingo ("Right on!") leave no doubt that this was produced in the seventies, but Essra Mohawk's spirited rendition overcomes any mustiness.

This was Tom Yohe's "maiden" effort at writing lyrics.

FACTS:

First Aired in 1976
Lyrics by Tom Yohe
Music by Bob Dorough
Performed by Essra Mohawk
Designed by Paul Kim and Lew Gifford
Animation by Kim and Gifford Productions

THREE-RING GOVERNMENT

SYNOPSIS

A young boy dreams of having a three-ring circus and then realizes it's just like the government . . . with Ring #1 being the ringmaster president, Ring #2, the acrobatic Congress, and Ring #3, the lion-taming Supreme Court.

Gonna have a three-ring circus someday,
People will say it's a fine one, son.
Gonna have a three-ring circus someday,
People will come from miles around.
Lions, tigers, acrobats, and jugglers and clowns galore,
Tightrope walkers, pony riders, elephants, and so much more . . .

Guess I got the idea right here at school.
Felt like a fool when they called my name,
Talkin' about the government and how it's arranged,
Divided in three like a circus.
Ring one, Executive,
Two is Legislative, that's Congress.
Ring three, Judiciary.
See it's kind of like my circus, circus.

Step right up and visit ring number one.
The show's just begun. Meet the President.
I am here to see that the laws get done.
The ringmaster of the government.

On with the show!

Hurry, hurry, hurry to ring number two.
See what they do in the Congress.
Passin' laws and juggling bills,
Oh, it's quite a thrill in the Congress.
Focus your attention on ring number three.
The Judiciary's in the spotlight.
The courts take the law and they tame the crimes
Balancing the wrongs with your rights.

No one part can be
more powerful than any other is.
Each controls the other you see,
and that's what we call checks and balances.

Well, everybody's act is part of the show.
And no one's job is more important.
The audience is kinda like the country you know,
Keeping an eye on their performance.

Ring one, Executive,
Two is Legislative, that's Congress.
Ring three, Judiciary.
See it's kind of like my circus, circus.

Gonna have a three-ring circus someday.
People will say it's a fine one son,
But until I get it, I'll do my thing
With government. It's got three rings.

TRIVIA

This segment on our government's system of checks and balances was made but not aired for several years out of concern that some politicians might be offended by the circus analogy.

FACTS

First Aired in 1979
Lyrics and Music by Lynn Ahrens
Performed by Lynn Ahrens
Designed by Arnold Roth
Animation by Phil Kimmelman
  and Associates

I'M JUST A BILL!

SYNOPSIS

When the folks back home decide that school buses should have to stop at railroad crossings, they call their local congressman, Representative McCoy, who agrees wholeheartedly: "You're right. There oughta be a law."

McCoy sends the little scrap of paper through the zigzag maze of the legislative process, where the bill is debated and voted on by both the House and the Senate before heading off to the White House with all the other bills (including a young "Billy").

All the hopeful dreaming of becoming a law makes for one worrisome Bill. Of course this lesson on how a bill becomes a law has a veto-less ending, and the president signs Bill, resulting in a joyous celebration.

BOY: Whew! You sure gotta climb a lot of steps to get to this Capitol Building here in Washington. But I wonder who that sad little scrap of paper is?

I'm just a bill.
Yes, I'm only a bill.
And I'm sitting here on Capitol Hill.
Well, it's a long, long journey
To the capital city.
It's a long, long wait
While I'm sitting in committee,
But I know I'll be a law some day
At least I hope and pray that I will
But today I am still just a bill.

BOY: Gee, Bill, you certainly have a lot of patience and courage.
BILL: Well, I got this far. When I started I wasn't even a bill, I was just an idea. Some folks back home decided they wanted a law passed, so they called their local Congressman, and he said, "You're right, there oughta be a law." Then he sat down and wrote me out and introduced me to Congress. And I became a bill, and I'll remain a bill until they decide to make me a law.

I'm just a bill
Yes I'm only a bill,
And I got as far as Capitol Hill.
Well, now I'm stuck in committee
And I'll sit here and wait
While a few key Congressmen discuss and debate
Whether they should let me be a law.
How I hope and pray that they will,
But today I am still just a bill.

BOY: Listen to those Congressmen arguing! Is all that discussion and debate about you?

BILL: Yeah, I'm one of the lucky ones. Most bills never even get this far. I hope they decide to report on me favorably, otherwise I may die.

BOY: Die?

BILL: Yeah, die in committee. Ooh, but it looks like I'm gonna live! Now I go to the House of Representatives, and they vote on me.

BOY: If they vote yes, what happens?

BILL: Then I go to the Senate and the whole thing starts all over again.

BOY: Oh no!

BILL: Oh yes!

I'm just a bill
Yes, I'm only a bill
And if they vote for me on Capitol Hill
Well, then I'm off to the White House
Where I'll wait in a line
With a lot of other bills
For the president to sign
And if he signs me, then I'll be a law.
How I hope and pray that he will,
But today I am still just a bill.

BOY: You mean even if the whole Congress says you should be a law, the president can still say no?

BILL: Yes, that's called a veto. If the president vetoes me, I have to go back to Congress and they vote on me again, and by that time you're so old . . .

BOY: By that time it's very unlikely that you'll become a law. It's not easy to become a law, is it?

BILL: No!

But how I hope and pray that I will,
But today I am still just a bill.

CONGRESSMAN: He signed you, Bill! Now you're a law!

BILL: Oh yes!!!

TRIVIA

It was 1975 when Bob Dorough suggested Dave Frishberg might be another resource for *SR* songs. A professional songwriter ("My Attorney, Bernie" and "Van Lingle Mungo," among others), Frishberg was living in L.A. at the time. Although he doesn't recall the precise chain of events that led to "I'm Just a Bill," he says he probably went to the library and checked out a few children's books about social studies.

But when he sat down to write the song, it was singer Jack Sheldon who came to mind. "It was his voice that I heard when I was writing the song," says Frishberg. "It was for Jack."

Once, when Frishberg was visiting a friend in the hospital and began reminiscing about "I'm Just a Bill," a voice from the next bed came drifting over the screen. It was a very ill man croaking out the words. "You never know where you're going to hear your songs," says Frishberg.

When Tom Yohe spoke at a senior symposium at Dartmouth College, a packed auditorium of students began singing it.

It is often requested by government groups and lobbyists to explain the complex process to staffers.

Jack Sheldon's son John is the voice of the little boy.

FACTS

First Aired in 1975
Lyrics and Music by Dave Frishberg
Performed by Jack Sheldon
Designed by Tom Yohe
Animation by Phil Kimmelman and Associates

Developed in Consultation with Dr. Odvard Egil Dyrli

TELEGRAPH LINE

SYNOPSIS

In this simple explanation of how the nervous system works, a telegram delivery boy traveling by bicycle hands telegrams to people in trouble. Remember the body made of power lines with human hands and feet? (Watch the foot when it falls asleep and snores . . . zzzzzz.)

Dit dittle dittle dit
Dit dittle dittle dit
Dittle dittle dit dit!

There's a telegram for you ma'am,
And the message is clear.
It says there's something bugging you
And buzzing in your ear.
The results can be quite itchy
So what is your reply?
Tell your arm to swat that fly!

Hey, there's a telegraph line,
You got yours and I got mine.
It's called the nervous system,
And everybody understands
Those telegram commands
And you know that everybody better listen!

The central nervous system
Is the brain and the spine.
The brain controls the system
And the spine is the line.
Telegrams come in
To tell what's happening to you,
Then telegrams go out
To tell your body what to do.

Dit dittle dittle dit
Dit dittle dittle dit
Dit dittle dittle dit

There's a telegram for you sir,
Better read it on the spot.
It says your hand is near a stove
That's very, very hot.
The results can be quite painful,
And there's no time to think,
Quick! Pull that hand away, and get it to the sink!

There's a telegraph line,
You got yours and I got mine.
It's called the nervous system,
And everybody understands
Those telegram commands
And you know that everybody better listen!

Your peripheral nerves,
They go all out,
Delivering those messages
Your senses send out.
From your hearing and touch
To your sight and taste and smell,
They let your brain react
To all the messages they tell.

Dit dittle dittle dit
Dit dittle dittle dit
Dit dittle dittle dit

There's a telegram for you, kid,
And it's at an awful time.
It says you've gotta go on stage
And you forgot your lines
You're gonna be embarrassed,
'Cause this telegram's a rush.
Your heart starts beatin' faster and you blush!

Hey, there's a telegraph line,
You got yours and I got mine.
It's called the nervous system,
And everybody understands
Those telegram commands
And you know that everybody better listen!

The autonomic system
Has a hold of you,
Controlling automatically
Some things that you do.
Your breathing and your heartbeat
Just go on naturally
And when you're scared, your nerves
Rev up the speed!

Dit dittle dittle dit
Dit dittle dittle dit
Dit dittle dittle dit

Hey, there's a telegraph line,
You got yours and I got mine.
It's called the nervous system,
And everybody understands
Those telegram commands
And you know that everybody better listen!

Dit dittle dittle dit
Dit dittle dittle dit
Dittle dittle dit dit!

TRIVIA

Animation designers are sparked by all sorts of things: The fancy bicycle riding at the end of this tune was inspired by Paul Newman's bike-riding scene in *Butch Cassidy and the Sundance Kid*.

On several occasions, this segment has been requested by medical schools to show first-year students a simple visual explanation of the nervous system.

FACTS

First Aired in 1979
Lyrics and Music
   by Lynn Ahrens
Performed
   by Jaime Aff and
   Christine Langner
Designed by Tom Yohe
Animation by
   Kim & Gifford
   Productions

DO THE CIRCULATION

SYNOPSIS

Remember when jogging was all the rage? . . .

Wearing an I ♥ NY sweatshirt, a young woman wakes up at 7:00 A.M. to go jogging in this tribute to the circulation system. Joggers in red and blue outfits give an aerial view of blood circulating through arteries and veins, taking nutrients to the cells, removing CO_2 waste, and knocking out germs with white blood cells.

There's a great new craze
That's sweeping the nation
Come on do the Circulation

It starts with your heart,
What a great sensation,
Come on do the Circulation!

Out through your arteries,
    in through your veins,
Your heart pumps your blood,
    then it does it again,
So come on, everyone get it on,
Everyone, the Circulation!
So come on, everybody,
Exercise your body for circulation!

Circulation! Everybody form a circle now, uh-huh-huh
Circulation! Like your blood, you just start moving around
Circulation! It's a function that's so out of sight
And if your feet fall asleep then
You're not circulating right.

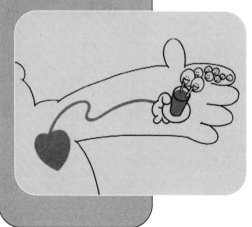

You got four heart parts to pump the blood (lub dub!)
Yeah, that's circulation,
Left and right ventricle, left and right atrium,
Yeah, they do it, they circulate,
They pump blood through your lungs for oxygen,
And then your arteries take it through to your body
And your veins bring the old blood back to be renewed.

Circulation takes nutrition to your cells
And gets rid of carbon dioxide and waste as well.
Circulation, it's a function that's so out of sight,
And if your hands are cold then
You're not circulating right.

Well, your blood is such a life-giving potion.
Like a river it's always in motion,
From your head to your toes,
Doing good as it goes,
It's a big, red, beautiful ocean.

Now the blood's not bad, it's kind of special,
Yeah, come dig it! Circulation!
With these red and white corpuscle cells,
Yeah, come do it, Circulation!
Red cells carry oxygen, white cells fight the germs,
So come on, come do it, yeah, come do it, Circulation!
So come on, come do it, with your heart, come do it, Circulation!

Circulation! Everybody form a circle now, uh-huh-huh.
Circulation! Like your blood, you just start moving around.
Circulation! It's a function that's so out of sight,
So come on, move around and
You'll be circulating right!

There's a great new craze that's sweeping the nation
Come on, do the Circulation!
It starts with your heart, what a great sensation.
Yeah, come do it, circulate!
Out through your arteries, in through your veins,
Your heart pumps your blood then it does it again.
Come on, everybody, get it on, everybody.
Circulation!
So come on, everybody, get it on, everybody.
Circulation!

The Circulation!

TRIVIA

Science Rock really challenged the designers. Dr. Gil Dyrli was a big help to Tom Yohe, Jack Sidebotham, and Lew Gifford—both in explaining scientific principles and in offering visual suggestions.

FACTS

First Aired in 1979
Lyrics and Music by Lynn Ahrens
Performed by Joshie Armstead, Mary Sue Berry,
    and Maeretha Stewart
Designed by Tom Yohe
Animation by Phil Kimmelman and Associates

THE BODY MACHINE

SYNOPSIS

This lesson in basic physiology and nutrition takes you step-by-step and organ-by-organ through the digestive system—from your esophagus to your small intestine—visualizing the various digestive processes along the way.

When you look down the street, what do you see?
The street is overflowing with a lot of machines.
Now I don't mean the buses, the trucks or cars.
I'm talking about the people,
Yeah, you know who they are.

I'm a machine, you're a machine.
Everybody that you know
You know, they are machines.
To keep your engine running you need energy
For your high-powered, revved-up body machine.
Your high-powered, revved-up body machine.

Now, I'd be a fool, if I said that the fuel that
We needed to burn was gasoline,
Because the fuel we use is the stuff called food,
And it puts out the power for our machine.
You make a stop at the filling station,
"Fill 'er up! One chicken sandwich to go!"
As you start to chew,
Your body does it. All systems go!

CHEF: Now that sandwich contains some very important kinds of food energy
for your body. The chicken gives you protein; bread, carbohydrates;
mayonnaise, fat; and the lettuce has vitamins, plus cellulose (or roughage).
Together these things help keep your body machine running smoothly.

First the saliva, kind of like a driver
"Move to the rear of the mouth!"
But what it's doing,
Along with teeth chewing,
Is taking food and breaking it down.

Down to the stomach,
The food is pushed, the esophagus does its stuff,
And the stomach starts,
Look at those moving parts,
As the body machine churns up
Gastric juices operate on proteins,
Fats and carbohydrates.

In the stomach they do what they do.
They take out the nutrition and use it for you.
And the cellulose, in those leaves you know,
Will control the traffic flow.
Helps the food to move along so the good stays in,
And the bad gets goin'.

I'm a machine, you're a machine.
Everybody that you know
You know they are machines.
To keep your engine running you need energy
For your high-powered, revved-up body machine.
Your high-powered, revved-up body machine.

Then the small intestine does most of your digesting,
By sending all the nutrients
In through the villi,
Which look a little silli
But act as little vents
The blood stream passes; the nutrients it catches
And takes them to the cells you see,
You use what it delivers,
And it stores some in the liver
For future energy.

I'm a machine, you're a machine.
Everybody that you know,
You know, they are machines.
To keep your engine running you need energy
For your high-powered, revved-up body machine.
Your high-powered, revved-up body machine.
Your high-powered, revved-up body machine.
High-powered, revved-up, complicated tune-up,
Fascinating body machine.

Take care of that machine.
You got such a great model there, honey!
Give it the right fuel
High protein, low calorie
Take it out for a spin every day!

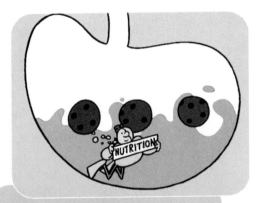

TRIVIA

Getting rid of "the waste" was a difficult task (visually) for the designer, but Lynn's lyrics " . . . will control the traffic flow" finally conjured up a body cop to help "the food to move along . . . "

FACTS

First Aired in 1979
Lyrics and Music by Lynn Ahrens
Performed by Bob Dorough
    and Jack Sheldon
Designed by Tom Yohe
Animation by Phil Kimmelman
    and Associates

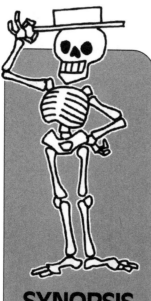

THEM NOT-SO-DRY BONES

SYNOPSIS

An all-male barbershop quartet explains the skeletal system by stepping out of their bodies and scaring each other with their skeletons.

Shows what a blob you'd look like without your bones, the "framework" that provides a rack to support and protect your vital organs and to hang your flesh on.

Them bones, them bones, them dry bones,
Now they're the working of the Lord.

Bones are heard of, but seldom seen,
'Cept each year 'round Halloween.
But I've got a shockeroo,
Right now there's a skeleton locked up inside of you. (Ha-ha-ha)

Minus bones you're just a blob,
Being framework's their main job.
All your organs, muscles, too,
They need your bones to hold them safe and sound inside for you.
Your heart and lungs are tucked away,
In there behind your ribs.
Those bones have been protecting them
Since we were little kids.
Lookout, here comes a bonehead play!
Birdin' his brain, (Tweet, tweet, tweet) what a day!
Don't take much to overwhelm it,
But luckily those bones up there work like a built-in helmet!
Shin bone connected to the knee bone
(That means the tibia connects to the patella)
Knee bone connected to the thigh bone
(That means the patella connects to the femur)
And here's how they really fit together.
Ligaments are what link bone to bone.
Cartilage that cushions in between.
Muscles hook on, by the tendons,
So here's what's happenin' in your knees most ev'ry time you bend 'em.

Now there's a lot of skeleton
We never get to see,
But it holds other little parts
That show quite obviously.
I'm talkin' 'bout those thirty-two
That we all call our teeth.
We gotta feed 'em right and keep 'em clean,
Or they can come to grief. (Ouch!)

So please remember,
You got to do it while you're young
Feed your bones some good old calcium
Drinking milk—a glass or two—
Will help your bones to stay in shape and do their job for you.

(Your skeleton)
It's a framework, (Yes, yes) holding you together.
Shielding organs, Yeah, that's its job, too!

TRIVIA

Originally called *Scholastic Rock*,
the series' name was changed to *Schoolhouse Rock*
when lawyers at Scholastic, Inc., a children's publisher,
put up a fuss.

FACTS:

First Aired in 1979
Lyrics and Music by George Newall
Performed by Jack Sheldon
Designed by Tom Yohe
Animation by Kim and Gifford Productions

A VICTIM OF GRAVITY

SYNOPSIS

A greaser sings a fifties-style doo-wop song blaming his clumsiness on the pull of the earth's gravity.

It's almost as though gravity has conspired to make him look less than "cool" in front of his girlfriend, Mary Jean.

After falling through a manhole, dropping his cheerleader girlfriend, and fumbling in football, he explains Newton's law of gravity and imagines the world without the powerful force: people, houses, trees, and pieces of ground all floating in the air.

Galileo and Isaac Newton make cameo appearances.

Down, down, down, down gravity

Helpin' wash the dishes
And I drop a cup.
Why does everything fall down
Instead of up?
Ridin' up a hill I spill
And hit the ground.
Wish I could fall up instead of always
    falling down.

Down, de-down, down, down.

I'm a victim of gravity.
Everything keeps fallin' down on me.
No matter where I go
That force is there I know,
Just a pullin' me down, down, down,
    down, down.
It's all around town now,
It's like a magnet deep inside
    the ground.
When I lift something up,
I can feel it pulling down.

It pulls me in the pool,
It pulls rain down on me.
I'm a victim of
Down, down, down, down, gravity, yeah.

Galileo, Galileo, Galilei—
He did experiments with a force
    he couldn't see.
(Could not see, yeah.)
He found that all things fall to earth
    at the very same speed
(Very same speed, yeah.)

He didn't know it yet, but that was due to gravity.
The moon goes 'round the earth
And shines its silver light.
The earth goes 'round the sun
And makes the seasons right.
It isn't love that makes the world go 'round, you see,
It's the power of gravity,
But please don't tell Mary Jean.
Down, de-down, down, down.

Without earth's gravity
To keep us in our place,
We'd have no weight at all,
We'd be in outer space.
The sea would float away,
And so would fields and towns,
Nothin' pullin' us down, down, down, down, down, yeah.

Isaac Newton underneath the apple tree.
(Apple tree, yeah)
One hit him on the head,
He said, "That must be gravity."

Newton's law of gravity says that every object in the universe
pulls on every other object. The bigger the object, the stronger
the pull. But the greater the distance between the objects, the
weaker the pull becomes.

Come back, Mary Jean!

Don't call me clumsy,
Don't call me a fool.
When things fall down on me,
I'm following the rule;
The rule that says that what goes up, comes down, like me,
I'm a victim of down, down, down, down gravity.

Shoo-be doo, down, down, down.

TRIVIA

Newton getting hit on the head with
an apple became the billboard for
Science Rock.

The Tokens skateboarded into the
studio to record this tune. Their hit song,
"The Lion Sleeps Tonight," had been
released a few years earlier.

FACTS

First Aired in 1978
Lyrics and Music by Lynn Ahrens
Performed by The Tokens
Designed by Tom Yohe
Animation by Kim and Gifford Productions

THE ENERGY BLUES

SYNOPSIS

A mournful Earth with a cloudy "hairpiece" sings the blues about the depletion of his natural resources, overcrowding, and the immense pollution people have created, while urging us to conserve and look for cleaner sources of energy.

(Yawn)

Energy . . .
Sometimes I think I'm running out of energy
Seems like we use an awful lot for
Heatin' and lightin' and drivin'
Readin' and writin' and jivin'
Energy . . . You'd think we'd be saving it up.

Energy . . . You can get it by dammin' up a river
Energy . . . A windmill can make the breeze deliver
But even with millin' and dammin'
Our needs are so much more demanding
For energy . . . We have to use some kind of fuel.

Chop, chop, chop, the cavemen used wood to start their fires.
Chop, chop, chop, they made all the tools that they required.
Chop, chop, chop, inventions got more and more inspired.
The fires got higher and higher,
And clearings got wider and wider.
Energy . . . They were burnin' 'bout all their wood up.

Then one day men discovered that coal would do it better
Miners dug, and it looked like it might just last forever.
It seemed like the final solution.
It started the Industrial Revolution.
Energy . . . We could just keep on diggin' it up.

Now in 1859—way out in western Pennsylvania—
A man had built a rig that got some laughs from folks who came there
But suddenly, a mighty roar came up from under the ground.

And soon a gusher, gushing oil, soaked all who stood around.
Now no one knew, when that gusher blew,
The petroleum years were on us,
Or that so many cars and trucks would come and cause a crisis.

Energy . . . We're looking to try and find some new kinds.
Energy . . . Exploring to try and make a new find.
Nuclear and thermal and solar,
If we miss we'll get colder and colder.
Energy . . . We've gotta stop usin' you up.

So don't be cross when Mama says turn that extra light out.
Just turn it off till we find us a fuel that never runs out.
If everyone tries a bit harder,
Our fuel will go farther and farther.
Energy . . . we're gonna be stretchin' you out.

TRIVIA

George Newall was serving as creative director on a major oil company account at the time he wrote this song, so the issues of the energy crisis were not exactly new to him.

Don't miss the Newall Coal Co.!

[There was originally another *Science Rock* song about the weather, but due to a pending lawsuit, we weren't able to include it in this collection.]

FACTS

First Aired in 1978
Lyrics and Music by George Newall
Performed by Jack Sheldon
Designed by Tom Yohe
Animation by Kim and Gifford Productions

ELECTRICITY, ELECTRICITY

SYNOPSIS

In this flashy spot, electricity gives us light to expose people and their actions (particularly burglars), and it enables us to shock our friends (or in this case, a sheep) with static electricity we get from petting a cat, using a comb, or walking across a carpet. The strobing electricity image makes for jolting fun.

When you're in the dark and you want to see,
You need uh . . . Electricity, Electricity
Flip that switch and what do you get?
You get uh . . . Electricity, Electricity
Every room can now be lit
With just uh . . . Electricity, Electricity

Where do you think it all comes from
This powerful . . . Electricity, Electricity
Through high wires to here it comes,
They're bringing uh . . . Electricity,
    Electricity

Every building must be wired to use it,
Uh . . . Electricity, Electricity

Power plants most all use fire to make it,
Uh . . . Electricity, Electricity

Burnin' fuel and usin' steam,
They generate . . . Electricity, Electricity

Turn that generator by any means,
You're making uh . . . Electricity, Electricity

A generator is a machine that contains a powerful magnet that creates a magnetic field. When wires are rotated rapidly through this field then a current of electricity is produced.

Now, if we only had a superhero who could stand here and turn the generator real fast, then we wouldn't need to burn so much fuel to make . . . electricity.

Benjamin Franklin flying his kite
Was searching for . . . Electricity, Electricity.
He knew that it had somethin' to do with lightnin',
It's all uh . . . Electricity, Electricity.

Rubbin' a comb with wool or fur will give you a charge of
Electricity (static) Electricity

Strokin' a cat to make it purr, you're buildin' up static
Electricity, Electricity

Electricity at rest is called static electricity.
Like in the winter wearing a heavy coat,
You get a shock off the doorknob.
Or you scrape across a carpet
And sneak up on your very best friend,
And zap 'im on the ear with a shock of—
Electricity, Electricity

Current flowing to and fro, makes a circuit of
Electricity, Electricity.
Voltage is the pressure that makes it go.
It's pushin' uh . . . Electricity, Electricity . . .

Watts will tell you just how much
You'll be usin'
Uh . . . Electricity, Electricity.

Powerful stuff, so watch that plug! It's potent
Electricity, Electricity.
Electricity, Electricity.

TRIVIA

The designers, Paul Kim and Lew Gifford, and
the animator, Al Eugster, gave the titles a
real "electrical" quality by utilizing short
single-frame cuts, flashing from nega-
tive to positive.

FACTS

First Aired in 1979
Lyrics and Music by Bob Dorough
Performed by Zachary Sanders
Designed by Paul Kim and Lew Gifford
Animation by Kim and Gifford Productions

INTERPLANET JANET

SYNOPSIS

This introduction to our solar system features Interplanet Janet, a cute, young "alien" with a space shuttle body, soaring across the cosmos with her comet team of ballplayers.

Janet starts her journey by visiting the sun (and getting an autograph) and then briefly stops by each planet until she finally gets to little Pluto on the outer reaches of our solar system.

They say our solar system is centered 'round the sun,
Nine planets, large and small, parading by.
But somewhere out in space,
There's another shining face
That you might see some night up in the sky.
Interplanet Janet, she's a galaxy girl,
A solar system Ms. from a future world,
She travels like a rocket with her comet team
And there's never been a planet Janet hasn't seen,
No, there's never been a planet Janet hasn't seen.

Interplanet Janet

She's been to the sun, it's a lot of fun,
It's a hot spot, it's a gas!
Hydrogen and helium in a big, bright, glowing mass.
It's a star, it's a star! So Janet got an autograph!

Mercury was near the sun so Janet stopped by,
But the mercury on Mercury was much too high, so
Janet split for Venus but on Venus she found
She couldn't see a thing for all the clouds around.
Earth looked exciting, kind of green and inviting,
So Janet thought she'd give it a go.
But the creatures on that planet looked so very weird to Janet,
She didn't even dare to say hello.

It's a bird, it's a plane! Why, it must be a UFO, but it was:
Interplanet Janet, she's a galaxy girl,
A solar system Ms. from a future world,
She travels like a rocket with her comet team
And there's never been a planet Janet hasn't seen,
No, there's never been a planet Janet hasn't seen.

Mars is red and Jupiter's big
And Saturn shows off its rings.
Uranus is built on a funny tilt
And Neptune is its twin,
And Pluto, little Pluto is the farthest planet from our sun.

They say our solar system is not alone in space.
The universe has endless mystery.
Some future astronaut
May find out that what he thought
Was a shooting star instead turned out to be . . .

Interplanet Janet, she's a galaxy girl,
A solar system Ms. from a future world,
She travels like a rocket with her comet team
And there's never been a planet Janet hasn't seen,
There's never been a planet Janet hasn't seen.

SHE'S A GALAXY GIRL!

TRIVIA

Probably the most popular *Science Rock* hit. Like "Conjunction Junction," its rhyming title is difficult to forget.

Lynn Ahrens had a niece and a nephew who would help her sing demos to her songs, and they sang the original demo of "Interplanet Janet" with her.

FACTS

First Aired in 1978
Lyrics and Music by Lynn Ahrens
Performed by Lynn Ahrens
Designed by Jack Sidebotham
Animation by Kim and Gifford Productions

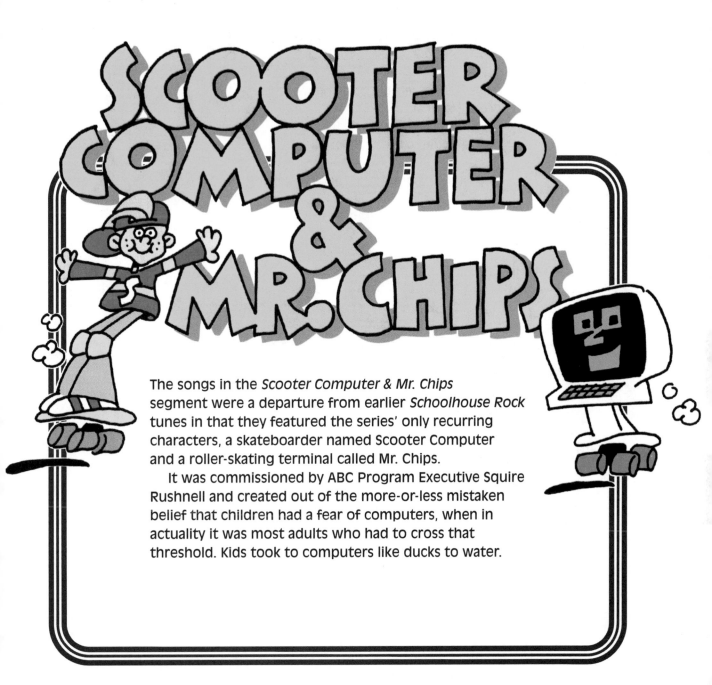

SCOOTER COMPUTER & MR. CHIPS

The songs in the *Scooter Computer & Mr. Chips* segment were a departure from earlier *Schoolhouse Rock* tunes in that they featured the series' only recurring characters, a skateboarder named Scooter Computer and a roller-skating terminal called Mr. Chips.

It was commissioned by ABC Program Executive Squire Rushnell and created out of the more-or-less mistaken belief that children had a fear of computers, when in actuality it was most adults who had to cross that threshold. Kids took to computers like ducks to water.

Developed in Consultation with Dr. Odvard Egil Dyril

INTRODUCTION

SYNOPSIS

A kid on a skateboard sings about all the terrific things the family's new computer can do for them.

When school lets out I race right home.
I'm faster than the bus,
I just can't wait to see my friend,
Who's come to live with us.

He's quite unique this friend of mine,
Like none you've ever seen.
He's full of fancy circuitry,
Instead of fingers he has keys,
And where a normal face should be he's got a special screen.

Scooter Computer and Mr. Chips
They've got the answers at their fingertips.
Scooter Computer and Mr. Chips
They've got the answers at their fingertips.

Mr. Chips is quite a whiz, he works with lightning speed.
He gives me information and the answers that I need.
He's got a super memory, but I'm what makes him tick.
He's programmed so that he reacts when I feed him data,
Those are facts, he sorts them out and answers back,
You ought to see how quick!

Anything you can do with paper and pencil I can do faster.

Scooter Computer and Mr. Chips
They've got the answers at their fingertips.
Scooter Computer and Mr. Chips
They've got the answers at their fingertips.

OK Mr. Chips let's show
These kids how much we know.

I type my questions on his keys to set my pal in motion.
Name the states that border on the great Pacific Ocean.

He's sure to have the answers
    if the program all was right.
He searches on his data crew,
And feeds back names of four or two.

I knew I could depend on you.
Hey Chips, you're out of sight.

It was nothing.

There's just no end to what we do
    with Mr. Chips around.
He helps me with my homework
    so I really get it down.
He prints the checks that pay the bills,
He stores up dates and names,
He files facts, makes shopping lists,
He tells us birthdays not to miss,
And then on top of all of this he's great at playing games.

Scooter Computer and Mr. Chips
They've got the answers at their fingertips.
Scooter Computer and Mr. Chips
They've got the answers at their fingertips.

TRIVIA

Although songwriters originally proposed their own ideas for songs, by the time *Scooter Computer & Mr. Chips* was developed, the creative team was assigning subjects to songwriters.

FACTS:

First Aired in 1983
Lyrics by Tom Yohe
Music by Bob Dorough
Performed by Jaime Aff and Bob Kaliban
Designed by Tom Yohe
Animation by Kim and Gifford Productions

SOFTWARE

SYNOPSIS

The basics of BASIC,
bits, and bytes.

To have some fun or pass a quiz,
Just follow this computer whiz.
Scooter Computer and Mr. Chips,
They've got the answers at their fingertips.

Here I am and there you stand, such distance in between,
'Cause I am a human and you are a machine.
How can I communicate exactly what I mean,
When I am a human and you are a machine?

Parlez-vous français?
Habla español?

I am a computer with so much in store,
If you could learn my language or I could speak in yours,
Then I'd do more work for you than you could ever dream.

Though you are a human and I am a machine.

OK., I'll give it a try.

First I hope you'll clear your mind and listen closely, Scooter.
Forget the words you thought you knew and start to think computer—
Computers change the letters and the numerals humans type
To a number code made up of things that we call bits and bytes.

Bits and bytes?

Think computer Scooter.
A byte is several digits all standing in a row,
They help present a letter or a number that you know.
For instance when you write an "A"
This byte is what I see,
And 00110011 is my way of saying "3."

This bit is one little bit of a byte.

I get it—bits and bytes are sort of a computer's alphabet.

That's right, but ABC and 123's isn't talking.
Hey let's face it
That's why one language that we use is called computer basic.

Computer basic?
"*B*eginner's *A*ll-purpose *S*ymbolic *I*nstruction *C*ode."
BASIC is a language that most computers know,
And once you start to speak it, communications flow.
You use words and phrases—I use bits and bytes instead, and BASIC lets us understand
what the other one just said. BASIC is a language that I can talk in human and you can
talk in machine and we can understand each other.

Yes, BASIC is the language you'll be using to feed in my data. It's also the language all
my programs or software are written in.

Data, programs, software?

Data is information.
Data means the facts.
It's everything you store in me
For solving problems back.
A program means directions
That tell me what to do,
How to analyze my data
And find answers just for you.
And software is just another name for
    all the instructions of programs
    that you feed me.

Here I am and there you stand, we're closer
    than we seem.
Though I am a human and you are a machine.
I'll get a book on BASIC and as quickly as I can
I will talk computer, and you will understand.

We didn't do too badly, did we Mr. Chips?

It was pretty amazing, Scooter.

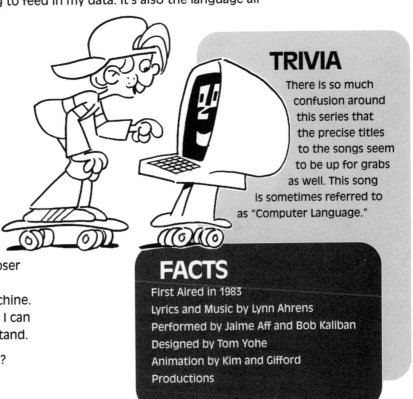

TRIVIA

There is so much confusion around this series that the precise titles to the songs seem to be up for grabs as well. This song is sometimes referred to as "Computer Language."

FACTS

First Aired in 1983
Lyrics and Music by Lynn Ahrens
Performed by Jaime Aff and Bob Kaliban
Designed by Tom Yohe
Animation by Kim and Gifford
Productions

HARDWARE

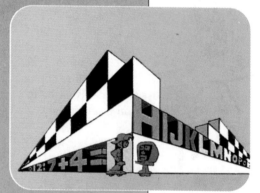

I beat you this time Mr. Chips. You're really good at these video games, but I can beat you sometimes.

Of course Scooter, because I'm no smarter than the person who programs me. After all, I'm only hardware, just like nuts and bolts.

Oh yeah, you're the smartest bag of nut and bolts I've ever seen.

Listen Scooter, some people assume that simply because a computer can gobble up all kinds of numbers and facts and figures and whatever data you happen to feed it, some people assume because a computer knows how to remember instructions and data and whatever it's told, and deliver it back whenever you need it as quick as a wink, some people assume a computer can think.

You mean you're not really so smart, Mr. Chips?

Right, Scooter, I'm not equipped to be smart. I'm not equipped to think. I'm equipped to use software and process information, not to understand it.

What's software?

The instruction you decide to give me.

And how do you use software?

I use software with my hardware. The terminal keyboard you touch when you want to say hi to me, that's hardware, my video screen when I want to reply to you, that's hardware too, and this complicated equipment crammed inside of me, too tiny for you to see, that's hardware, too.

Nothing but diodes, capacitors, and resistors, interconnections and transistors, jammed together like canned sardines, thousands of teeny, tiny machines, printed on miscroscopic strips called chips.

Chips . . . So that's why they call you . . .

Precisely.

Gee, Mr. Chips, you have a great brain!

Brain? No, Scooter, I have no brain. Some people assume that simply because I can beat them at math, and war games, and chess, and checkers, invaders and raiders, all in the same afternoon, some people assume because I can shoot off a rocket and chart it and clock it, control and command it and steer it and land it, precisely there on the moon—it's hard to explain, but some people assume I have a brain.

OK, but if you don't have a brain, how can you do so many different things?

Because of the different kinds of software people can feed me, scientists or secretaries; astronauts or accountants; managers or musicians; as long as it's put in a language I can understand, I can store the directions in my chips.

I assure you I haven't a brain and I haven't a heart,
And my chips would feel no pain if you took me apart,
And I'll never know good from bad, or black from white,
And I'll never know happy from sad or wrong from right.

I'm nothing but diodes, capacitors, and resistors, Interconnections and transistors, jammed together like canned sardines, thousands of teeny, tiny machines, printed on microscopic strips called chips. And it's all hardware just like nuts and bolts.

You're sure a smooth talker, Mr. Chips.

Maybe so, Scooter, but you're the brains of the operation.

TRIVIA

Although filed under the title "Hardware," this song has also come to be known as "Hardware and Software."

Dave Frishberg's assignment was to write a song about the actual mechanics and electronics of computing.

When Frishberg first sat down to write this song, he began by reading books George Newall sent him in the mail that explained what computers were all about. "I had to learn this stuff, too," says Frishberg.

FACTS

First Aired in 1983
Lyrics and Music by Dave Frishberg
Performed by Jaime Aff and Bob Kaliban
Designed by Paul Kim and Lew Gifford
Animation by Kim and Gifford Productions

NUMBER CRUNCHER

SYNOPSIS

A lesson on data processing.

Baseball's s'posed to be fun!
Can't wait to hit a home run,
But they got me playing the wrong position
Since they made me the statistician.
I'm in numbers up to my ears!
This is gonna take me years and years
And years and years and years.

MR. CHIPS: Numbers? Scooter, did you say numbers?
SCOOTER: Yes, numbers, Mr. Chips. Batting averages, earned run averages, team
   standings . . . I can probably figure this stuff out, but I'll miss batting practice.
MR. CHIPS: Feed me those numbers. I'll do the work.
SCOOTER: You mean . . .
MR. CHIPS: Precisely!

Sit down, Scooter, you're in for a treat.
Numbers, you see, are just my meat . . .

'Cause I'm a number cruncher
A mathematical muncher
I can round numbers off, I can square them
I can line numbers up and compare them
I can change them around, rearrange them around
I can deal with them in any way you choose

I'm not a math professor,
I am a data processor.
I can mix numbers up and combine them,
I can take them apart and align them.
I can shake numbers up, I can break numbers up,
I can turn them into something you can use.
If you can punch them,
I can crunch them
'Cause I'm a number cruncher.

SCOOTER: Mr. Chips, you're amazing!

MR. CHIPS: Elementary, Scooter. A piece of cake. Just feed me the numbers and I'll process them for you.

SCOOTER: In other words, I punch them . . .

MR. CHIPS: Precisely, and I crunch them

I process numbers as quick as a flash
For whatever results you need.
I process numbers into measuring tools
To measure sound and time and speed
I process numbers to find just how fast
A rocket can get to Mars.
I project the future and recall the past,
And I can show you a map of the stars.

SCOOTER: Wow!

I process numbers into curves and lines,
Display them on a graph or chart.
I process numbers into colors and shapes
To make a digital work of art!

. . . A work of art!

'Cause I'm a number cruncher,
A mathematical muncher.
I can round numbers off, I can square them,
I can line numbers up and compare them.
I can change them around, rearrange them around.
I can deal with them in any way you choose.

I'm not a math professor,
I am a data processor.
I can mix numbers up and combine them.
I can take them apart and align them.
I can shake numbers up, I can break numbers up,
I can turn them into something you can use.

SCOOTER: My baseball statistics?

MR. CHIPS: A piece of cake! But remember: First you have to punch them . . .

SCOOTER: I know . . . then you can crunch them . . . 'Cause you're a number cruncher!!!

MR. CHIPS: Precisely.

TRIVIA

Dave Frishberg said he found that the creative process was actually much easier when he was given a lot of rules and restrictions, as was the case with "Number Cruncher." But he did find it difficult when Tom Yohe created the characters—Scooter Computer and Mr. Chips. Frishberg wasn't thrilled with the idea of writing song lyrics for a computer, and he was puzzled by the fact that Scooter Computer was a boy, not a computer.

He has since written three new songs for *SR*'s *Money Rock* series. He also performs a solo act and has begun to sing excerpts from various *SR* songs.

FACTS

First Aired in 1984
Lyrics and Music by Dave Frishberg
Performed by Jaime Aff and Bob Kaliban
Designed by Paul Kim and Lew Gifford
Animation by Kim and Gifford Productions

Darn! *That's The End!*

The music's not exactly the way you remembered (but it's a whole lot easier to dance to)

SCHOOL HOUSE ROCK! ROCKS

THE ALBUM

New Versions of the Songs from the 70's smartest cartoons

Biz Markie

Blind Melon

Buffalo Tom

Chavez

Daniel Johnston

Deluxx Folk Implosion

Goodness

Lemonheads

Man Or Astro-Man?

Moby

Pavement

Skee-Lo

Ween

    THE ATLANTIC GROUP

TO ORDER BY PHONE...
1-800 ASK TOWER
RECORDS • VIDEO • BOOKS
...OR FOR STORE LOCATIONS

surf atlantic
http://www.atlantic-records.com

Available on CD and cassette

"Conjunction Junction, What's Your Function?"

If you don't recognize those five little words, then you weren't camped out in front of the television set every Saturday morning from 1973 to 1985. Those catchy, jazzy tunes from *Schoolhouse Rock* taught millions of us the fundamentals of math, grammar, science, and history. We learned how a bill becomes a law in "I'm Just a Bill," the planets of our solar system in "Interplanet Janet," how to turn an adjective into a perfectly good adverb in "Lolly, Lolly, Lolly, Get Your Adverbs Here," and we unknowingly memorized the Preamble to the Constitution!

A blast from the past, *SCHOOLHOUSE ROCK! The Official Guide* includes all the unforgettable lyrics and memorable moments from the forty original segments, including:

My Hero, Zero	Telegraph Line
Three Is a Magic Number	A Victim of Gravity
Figure Eight	Interplanet Janet
Conjunction Junction	Sufferin' Till Suffrage
Lolly, Lolly, Lolly, Get Your Adverbs Here	The Preamble
Interjections!	I'm Just a Bill

Sprinkled with facts and behind-the-scenes trivia, *SCHOOLHOUSE ROCK! The Official Guide* is the must-have book for every fan who wants to relive this beloved, pop culture sensation.

George Newall *(right)* was an executive at the McCaffrey & McCall advertising agency when he was asked to put the multiplication tables to music. Fellow advertising man Tom Yohe *(left)* created the visuals and the rest is history. Both are still producing new segments for the series, which ABC revived in 1993 and now airs every Saturday morning.

HYPERION

ISBN 0-7868-8170-4
50995

EAN

9 780786 881703

**MULTIPLICATION ROCK, AMERICA ROCK, SCIENCE ROCK, AND GRAMMAR ROCK
ARE NOW AVAILABLE ON VIDEO FROM ABC VIDEO!**